T0042861

REMEMBER
MY
STORY

✦

REMEMBER MY STORY

A GIRL, A HOLOCAUST SURVIVOR, AND A FRIENDSHIP THAT MADE HISTORY

Claire Sarnowski
with **Sarah Durand**

LITTLE, BROWN AND COMPANY
New York Boston

Little, Brown and Company
Hachette Book Group
1290 Avenue of the Americas, New York, NY 10104
Visit us at LBYR.com

First Edition: January 2024

Little, Brown and Company is a division of Hachette Book Group, Inc. The Little, Brown name and logo are trademarks of Hachette Book Group, Inc.

The publisher is not responsible for websites (or their content) that are not owned by the publisher.

Little, Brown and Company books may be purchased in bulk for business, educational, or promotional use. For information, please contact your local bookseller or the Hachette Book Group Special Markets Department at special.markets@hbgusa.com.

Library of Congress Cataloging-in-Publication Data
Names: Sarnowski, Claire, author. | Durand, Sarah, author.
Title: Remember my story : a girl, a Holocaust survivor, and a friendship that made history / Claire Sarnowski with Sarah Durand.
Other titles: Girl, a Holocaust survivor, and a friendship that made history
Description: First edition. | New York : Little, Brown and Company, 2024. | Audience: Ages 8–12 | Summary: "The true story of a young girl and a Holocaust survivor whose friendship led to a significant change in their community and beyond." —Provided by publisher.
Identifiers: LCCN 2023004015 | ISBN 9780316592895 (hardcover) | ISBN 9780316592840 (ebook)
Subjects: LCSH: Wiener, Alter, 1926-2018—Juvenile literature. | Holocaust survivors—Oregon—Hillsboro—Biography—Juvenile literature. | Sarnowski, Claire—Juvenile literature. | Holocaust, Jewish (1939–1945)—Study and teaching—Oregon—Juvenile literature. | Holocaust, Jewish (1939–1945)—Personal narratives—Juvenile literature. | Jews—Poland—Biography—Juvenile literature. | Teenage girls—Oregon—Lake Oswego—Biography—Juvenile literature. | Teenagers—Oregon—Lake Oswego—Biography—Juvenile literature. | Lake Oswego (Or.)—Biography—Juvenile literature. | Hillsboro (Or.)—Biography—Juvenile literature.
Classification: LCC DS134.72.W54 S37 2024 | DDC 940.53/18092279541—dc23/eng/20230130
LC record available at https://lccn.loc.gov/2023004015

ISBNs: 978-0-316-59289-5 (hardcover), 978-0-316-59284-0 (ebook)

Printed in the United States of America

LSC-C

Printing 1, 2023

TO ALTER, WHO LIT A FIRE THAT
WILL NEVER GO OUT

CONTENTS

$\longrightarrow \blacklozenge \longrightarrow$

There are two ways to deal with the cold—put on a coat to be warm or light a fire so that others can be warm, too.

—RACHEL WURTZEL WIENER,
ALTER WIENER'S STEPMOTHER

A smart man is the one who learns from his experience, but still the smartest man is the one who learns from somebody else's experiences.

—ANONYMOUS

PART TWO: THIS IS FOR OUR FUTURE

PROLOGUE

—————◆—————

WHEN YOU'RE FOURTEEN YEARS OLD, THE ONE place you don't expect to be on a random weekday is standing in front of your state capitol building with a ninety-two-year-old Holocaust survivor you met four years earlier. But on a sunny September morning in 2018, that's exactly where I found myself. I wasn't on a field trip, at a Model Congress conference, or waiting to snap a selfie on a family vacation. I was missing school to testify in front of a committee of Oregon state senators, and I was so excited I thought my heart might burst out of my chest.

The man I was with was named Alter Wiener. I'd first met him when I was nine years old and attended a presentation he gave. Alter was a slender, white-haired Polish immigrant who had experienced more tragedy and loss than I could comprehend. Yet he was filled with so much joy and optimism that it was contagious—and, lucky for me, he had become my best friend.

It was a pretty unlikely friendship for a girl who had just started high school, but it *worked*, and Alter's influence had changed the course of my life.

Like so many of us born in the shadows of 9/11, I couldn't log on to the internet without sensing that my life was somehow connected to others across the world. But social media is not the real world, right? Instead of using those online connections to enact change, it felt like everyone in my community looked inward, toward our own needs. At school, we studied hard so we could get into good colleges, rushed to make it to dance or soccer practice on time, and texted our friends long after we should have turned the lights out. In the summer, we splashed in the lake and slept late, and nobody really worried about the war our country had been fighting since before we were born. If we did, it was something happening far, far away.

With Alter, it was different. War had destroyed his childhood, and by teaching me about it, he had taken me out of my comfort zone and made my life fuller. Through knowing him, I had become a catalyst for change, like he was. Instead of obsessing over Instagram, my grades, or Harry Styles (okay, maybe I'm lying about being over Harry—more on that later) now I spent most of my time furthering Alter's mission: raising awareness about the Holocaust.

Alter wasn't getting any younger, and he was *tired*. Over the course of nearly twenty years, he'd spoken to almost 1,000 community and school groups about the Holocaust and how remembering it could help prevent intolerance and violence. His words had made a lasting impact on so many people, young and old, but he was worried that when he was gone, Holocaust education would die as well.

I assured him: Not if I had anything to do with it.

Alter's message felt especially urgent in 2018, when our country was so culturally and politically divided. Worse than these divisions, though, was the all-out *hate*. In fact, there had recently been a few hate crimes in my hometown, Lake Oswego, Oregon. I thought that if more people knew Alter's story and understood the history of the Holocaust and other genocides, then maybe these acts of hostility would stop. Maybe, just maybe, tolerance would finally overtake violence.

Alter and I had spent months building a case to make Holocaust education mandatory in Oregon's public school curriculum. I'd researched other states' laws and curricula extensively, and I'd gotten out of bed at 6:00 AM—even on the weekends—to email parents, teachers, and community members about our efforts. Alter and I had written and called hundreds of his contacts, asking them for their stories and photos so we could add them to our presentations. We'd spent hours drumming up support for our cause and trying to get people to attend this meeting. If we could convince the Oregon State Senate Education Committee how urgent it was for students to learn about the Holocaust, then these seven senators would go to the full legislature and push to pass a bill.

With every bone in my body, I knew what was at stake. This bill was *everything*. But what if no one else cared?

I took a deep breath, looked toward Alter in his wheelchair, and began to help him up the ramp that led to the Oregon State Capitol Rotunda. Together, we'd made it this far. Together, we were going to change history.

PART ONE

MY BEST
FRIEND

Chapter One

A VERY TRUE STORY

Of the hundreds of people standing in the cafeteria of Crossler Middle School on May 30, 2014, I knew I was probably the youngest. I was nine years old, and the only reason I was skipping a day of fourth grade was that my aunt Sue taught at Crossler and she and my mom thought I'd be interested in the man who was there to speak: Alter Wiener, a Holocaust survivor.

They were right.

Alter Wiener was famous around the Portland, Oregon, metro area for sharing his experiences and educating people of all ages about the Holocaust. Aunt Sue had helped organize the event, and she'd saved me and my mom seats in the first row. When we reached our chairs, I sat down, adjusted my glasses, and looked just ahead of me. I'd finished Alter's memoir that week (my mom had bought it for us to read in advance of seeing him), but here he was, real and only a few feet away. He was slender and elderly and wore a dark suit and tie. His white hair hung in wisps at the sides of his head, his mouth was closed tight, and his dark, piercing eyes scanned the crowd. Next to him on the podium sat a water bottle and a laptop.

I'd never met a Holocaust survivor—Alter had written that western Oregon didn't exactly have large communities of European Jewish immigrants—but Mom had told me about the Holocaust when I was in first grade. I was barely six, and a big part of her worried that the subject would really upset me. But a bigger part of her thought it was important for me to understand even the worst parts of human history so I could learn from them. She described how she, Aunt Sue, and my grandparents had taken a trip to Germany when she was ten and Sue was twelve. They'd traveled ten miles outside of Munich—Germany's third largest city—to visit the concentration camp Dachau. She told me that seeing the cramped barracks and the memorials to the 41,500 people who'd been murdered inside the camp's walls has haunted her since then. But after that trip she vowed to become a better, more compassionate person— something she wanted me to grow up to be.

"When we forget about history, Claire," Mom said, "we're doomed to repeat it. I want you to understand that hate and intolerance led to millions of people being killed during World War Two, and that should *never* happen again."

When Alter Wiener stood up carefully that day and began to speak, it was clear he had the same goal my mom had: to talk about history so that we could avoid repeating it.

"What I'm going to tell you is not pleasant, but it's a very true story," he said in his heavy Polish accent. "I have no reason to exaggerate. I am not an actor."

Alter was eighty-seven, which was about ten years older than my grandparents were at the time. His movements were slow and deliberate, and his body tilted slightly to one side. He was also short, but he didn't look frail or weak. In fact, he delivered his words so confidently and steadily that it was hard to think of him as anything but strong. There was something powerful inside him that had held him together through incredibly brutal times.

As Alter continued talking, the last few noises in the room faded away, and for the next seventy minutes, he spoke almost without stopping. He told us that the Nazi army (the army for Germany's ruling political party during World War II) invaded Poland when he was thirteen, and he was forced to wear an armband with the Star of David. Nazis believed that anyone who was Jewish was inferior, and the armbands were a way to identify them easily. Officials closed his synagogue and made it illegal for Jews to worship, and Jewish children were forbidden to attend school. This new way of life meant that Alter couldn't travel, own a radio, go to the playground, or visit a theater, and he endured verbal attacks from non-Jews as he walked down the street.

But by far the cruelest thing was this: Within two weeks of the Nazis marching into Alter's hometown, soldiers shot his father and watched as he bled to death. Then they threw his body into a mass grave. Alter and his stepmother didn't find out where he was for two long, agonizing weeks, and when they went to identify his remains, Alter watched her collapse to the ground in shock.

"When I was fifteen," he continued, his Polish accent softening the way he pronounced the letter *s*, "I was deported to Blechhammer, a labor camp in southern Poland." He pivoted right, then left, his hands raised and gesturing animatedly. "This was my first camp, but it wouldn't be my last."

After Blechhammer, he moved around to four other camps until he was eighteen. For almost four years, Alter didn't see a woman, a child, or a blooming flower. He ate all his meals out of one metal bowl, with no forks or spoons to help him. He couldn't brush his teeth or comb his hair. He didn't eat a fruit or a vegetable. He didn't have a calendar, so he had no idea what day—or even year—it was. He wore wooden-soled shoes without socks, even on the coldest days of winter, and he slept without a blanket or sheets on a pile of straw that was infested with roaches and lice.

Alter shared each new piece of information about what his life was like in a matter-of-fact tone. But the weight of his words was not lost on anyone.

"The Nazis took away my name, too," he said, then paused as this sank in. "I became Number 64735 instead."

When the Russian army finally liberated Alter's camp on May 9, 1945, he was down to eighty pounds, and he had thick, dark circles under his eyes. He made his way back to his hometown, and there he discovered he didn't have an apartment anymore. So he walked unsteadily to the local cemetery, and he slept for three nights on his father's grave. He had no money for food or a clean bed, and he didn't have anyone to stay with, either. He didn't know it yet, but he'd soon discover that nearly every person in his 123-member family—except for him and a few cousins—had been murdered.

"Through all of this, though," Alter told us, his voice lifting and carrying through the room, "I've become better, not bitter."

My heart was already aching, but it started to feel like it weighed one hundred pounds as Alter pointed out people, places, and images on the PowerPoint slides projected onto the screen at the front of the cafeteria.

"This is my father, Mordechai-Markus Wiener," he said, motioning toward a young, bearded man dressed up in a hat, coat, and tie. "He's with my uncle and a family friend. This was taken sometime in the late 1930s. My daddy didn't live to see 1940."

Alter switched slides and pointed to his grand-mother. As I looked at her—this woman with a slight smile—I thought about how, in that moment, she had no idea that she'd be murdered in Auschwitz only a few years later. Then he scrolled through images of men digging their own graves and women without shoes clutching their children's hands as they walked into the gas chamber.

I grabbed my mom's arm. Alter hadn't put these last images in his book—only in the slideshow—and the grief that was washing over me felt unbearable. Shuddering, I finally looked up toward Alter. He was pacing near the podium, still talking without one note of self-pity.

"I always have hope," he said, his voice rising like he was about to break into song. "I could have died as a young man in the camps, but instead, I lived. Against all odds, I survived. Remember my story; it will remind you why you should never ever lose hope."

When Alter finished his speech, the room erupted

in applause. I looked behind me and saw a few kids dabbing their eyes and a handful of others who looked like they might burst into tears at any second. I wasn't crying. Instead, I was filled with a wave of hope that extended out of the cafeteria and right up into the stars. Here was this kind, brave soul who'd spoken for more than an hour about how he lost his childhood *and* his entire family, yet he didn't seem angry. He said he didn't want revenge. He just wanted people to understand what had happened in the past so they could educate others, spread messages of kindness, and never *ever* again stand by when they see something unspeakable happening.

Now I wanted that, too.

Chapter Two

MAKE THE WORLD A BETTER PLACE

"HI, I'M CLAIRE SARNOWSKI," I SAID, CAREFULLY pulling down the microphone that stood in the middle of the Crossler cafeteria. "I'm a fourth grader at River Grove Elementary—"

Alter interrupted me. "Nice to meet you, Claire. Did you enjoy the presentation?"

I must have blushed because Alter's mouth curled up into a kind, encouraging smile. "Oh—yes," I stammered, searching for the words that would show him how inspired I was. "I—I—loved every minute of it."

"Thank you for coming," he responded. "I'm glad you are here."

I nodded my head and straightened my glasses.

Even though I had rehearsed my question the night before, I was nervous. In fact, a few students had gone before me, and I'd been so busy saying the question to myself that I'm not sure I'd even heard them. "I wanted to ask you . . . What would you have done with your life if the Holocaust hadn't happened?"

Alter paused, then scrunched up his nose and eyebrows. "Thank you for your question, Claire," he said warmly, instantly reassuring me that I'd been fine. "I'm not sure what I would have done. I can't really imagine my life without the Holocaust because it changed everything. But I believe I would have done something that satisfied my heart and mind. I have always wanted to make the world a better place."

And you have, I thought.

After the question-and-answer session ended, Mom, Aunt Sue, and I walked toward Alter. Mom stood next to me, and she opened her purse, pulled out our copy of Alter's book, *From a Name to a Number*, and handed it to me.

"Hi, Mr. Wiener," I said. "Um, I was wondering… Can you sign a copy of your book for me?"

Alter nodded his head, then smiled. "Of course I can sign it," he answered. "I am honored you liked my book. Your question was excellent and very thought-provoking."

I smiled right back because I *so* badly wanted to talk more with him. I hardly knew Alter, but he had an energy that felt like it was making me grow inches and years by the second. Luckily, Aunt Sue had already asked me to ride with her while she drove Alter home.

A few minutes later, Alter got settled into the front seat of my aunt's car, and I moved into the back. I opened the small tote bag I'd carried with me. Right there next to a novel I was reading was a drawing I had made and was working up the nerve to give to him.

In his book, Alter had written about how, when he was imprisoned, he'd think about the blue skies and fields of flowers he'd grown up surrounded by in Poland. During restless, nightmare-filled sleeps on his straw mattress, he imagined the butterflies that used to soar over those fields. He decided that someday, if he ever got home, he'd never take nature for granted. He would never ever forget to be thankful for flowers and butterflies and big blue skies.

My picture was my best interpretation of what he'd imagined. I wasn't a great artist, but I'd put my heart and soul into it, carefully blending the colors so that the butterflies' wings looked soft, yet vibrant, and the clouds melted into a deep blue sky.

"Mr. Wiener, I made something for you," I said as I reached toward the front seat, holding the drawing in my hands. "It's like what you described in your book."

He looked at it for a few seconds before taking it from me. "Oh, Claire. This is one of the nicest gifts I've ever received. Thank you so much. And, please, call me Alter."

I breathed a sigh of relief. I just *knew* he'd like it.

The ride from Salem to Hillsboro, where Alter lived, was about an hour and twenty minutes. I had so many questions for him, so I started asking them, and before I knew it, we were trading stories. We covered everything: my friends, his friends, my parents and grandparents, his kids and grandkids, world events, the weather, our favorite books. . . . I mean, *everything*. It might seem weird that a nine-year-old and an eighty-seven-year-old could connect like we did, but Alter was just different. He was never condescending, and he listened to me. His energy was like a warm blanket or an old sweater, soft and comforting at all the right moments.

I think Aunt Sue liked seeing me so excited about something, so she kept mostly quiet as she drove. When we pulled into Alter's apartment complex, it felt too soon. Aunt Sue and I walked him to his front door, and for a split second, I was glad Alter moved slowly. I didn't want to say goodbye yet.

"Please, come in," he said, standing on his pink doormat as he turned his key in the lock. "Make yourselves comfortable."

I guess Alter didn't want to say goodbye yet, either.

Aunt Sue and I followed him inside, and we sat down at a square table in front of a large wall that had a built-in shelf. On the wall and shelf were diplomas, photos, and a framed letter he'd received from President Barack Obama.

"See?" he said, pointing to the wall. "I've received

an honorary bachelor's degree and an honorary law degree. I was banned from attending school in Poland when I was thirteen, but I got my high school equivalency in America when I was thirty-five because I went to night school...after I spent my days working as a janitor to afford the classes."

"You must have been so tired," I said. "After school and dance class, sometimes I'm so worn out I can't do my homework."

Alter laughed. "I was exhausted," he said. "But I had a wife and two young boys, and I wanted to give my family a good life."

I noticed that Alter had taken off his dress shoes and put on a pair of slippers. He moved carefully from the couch to his desk, then walked to the table holding a baseball cap with the title of his book on it.

"So you can remember me," he smiled, extending the hat toward me. I put it on right away. "Now, would you like some smoothies? After all the time I spent in the camps, I have digestive problems. I've become very interested in nutrition and find that smoothies really help me."

"I'm so sorry," my aunt said sympathetically. "But

if you're offering smoothies, Claire and I would love some."

As Alter shuffled over to his kitchen, I wondered if his small size was due to his age or the fact that he'd spent so many years without good nutrition. He'd written that while he was a prisoner, he ate snow and stole raw potato peels out of the trash. He even once traded his father's watch for a loaf of bread—and received fifty lashes with a whip for it. I guess I'd taken for granted all the food I had in my life. My family wasn't exactly rich, but I'd spent my entire life with three meals a day and a school that provided a hot lunch if Mom hadn't packed my lunch box for me.

A few moments later Alter emerged from the kitchen with three tall glasses on a tray. Each was filled to the brim with a thick pink liquid dotted with blue flecks. My aunt jumped up to help him.

"Here's to friendship," I said once everyone was seated, lifting my glass and clinking it with Alter's.

"Here's to friendship," he echoed.

And that was how it all started with me and my best friend.

Chapter Three

✦

ME BEFORE ALTER

When I was a little girl growing up in the suburbs, I loved school, dance practice, playing tennis, and hanging out with my friends and family. I was one of those kids who was rarely at a loss for words. I loved to talk, and I always had a hundred questions. I wanted to be a doctor when I grew up.

Life wasn't perfect, though. My mom had been diagnosed with multiple sclerosis (MS) nine years before I was born, and seeing her struggle could be tough. It also made me take life a little more seriously than a lot of kids my age did. My parents had always taught me that each day is precious and that we should all strive to take care of one another. They also taught me to give back, so we took part in Portland's fundraising walk for MS (called Walk MS) every year. When I was a baby, my mom or my dad pushed me along the way in a stroller, and when I was a toddler, I held their hands and walked between them.

Multiple sclerosis is a neurological disease that occurs when the immune system starts to attack your nerves. The damage that results messes up the communication between your brain and the rest of your body, causing people with MS to feel nerve pain, have difficulty moving, talk slowly, become extremely tired, experience numbness and tingling, or have trouble seeing. While every patient has a different experience, here's how I think of MS: It's like your brain calls the nerves in your foot, but the nerves in your hand answer instead.

At the many Walk MS days over the years, I'd met people with all types of MS and saw how it affected each of them. Some were in wheelchairs or had lost the ability to speak and write, and others, like my mom, lived their lives with only occasional health complaints.

Mom, Dad, and I loved doing Walk MS, and along the route my parents would talk about the importance of being compassionate and helping others. Mom explained that her disease hadn't progressed as fast as it could have because of the money people raised—which went to research for treatments and a possible cure—and that thought stuck with me. When I was four, Mom helped me call a few friends and family members who lived in other parts of the country and ask them to make pledges to the local branch of the National Multiple Sclerosis Society. Like most preschoolers, the concept of money *counting* for something didn't make much sense to me, but I understood Mom's message: Money helped make people with MS better. So on the weekends, I started walking around my neighborhood to solicit donations. Mom and Dad stood on the curb while I tiptoed up to my neighbors' doors, lifted my little fist, and knocked hard. When someone answered, I'd start talking as fast as I could.

"Hi! I'm Claire, from down the street. I'm raising money for multiple sclerosis research. This is a cause that's very important to me because my mom has MS. Would you be willing to give a donation? Any amount helps!"

I was just a kid, but I wasn't going to let that stop me

from doing something. That first year, I raised $900. I've fundraised almost every year since and have raised a total of over $100,000 for the National MS Society.

Not bad for just a kid!

My instinct to right wrongs didn't stop there, and my parents were always happy to support me in my efforts. When I was seven years old, I realized that some people didn't get Christmas gifts, so I raised money and bought toys for children at my local hospital. When I was eight, I used the money I made from selling handmade greeting cards to fund a Christmas for a family friend a few grades below me. She and her mom were having a bad year financially, so my mom and I shopped for gifts *and* decorated their house—top to bottom. And every year since then, I've donated to every single canned food drive and coat drive I can find.

When Alter said he wanted to make the world a better place, I realized something: That's what I had always wanted, too.

CHAPTER FOUR

MATZO BALL SOUP AND MEMORIES

Date: June 1, 2014, 4:19 PM
From: Claire Sarnowski
To: Alter Wiener

Mr. Wiener,

I haven't been able to get you or your wonderful talk out of my mind. I was very inspired by your moving story. I'm so sorry an amazing man like you had to endure the treatment that you have. I have always tried to be a good person and to love everybody but after I heard you speak I realized I need to make sure that your story and people like you are honored. I can't wait to get to school and share with my class the experience you gave me. I feel very privileged and honored that I got to accompany you and my aunt Sue to Hillsboro. Thank you so much for welcoming me into your lovely home. I really loved and appreciated the smoothie and hat. I will wear the hat with pride!

Hope to see you soon.

Please feel free to write me whenever at this email. If you need ANYTHING or if I can be any assistance to you please email me or feel free to call me. Please know you are my hero and I love you very much.

Love,
Claire Sarnowski

Some parents might think it was odd if their fourth grader struck up a friendship with an almost ninety-year-old. Not my mom. First, she'd already met Alter, so he had her stamp of approval. Second, she knew I'd always liked being around older people. As an only child, I lived in an adult world at home, with the news always on TV and conversations about current events at dinner. I was also super close to my grandma, and I visited her as often as I could at her house in Washington. When I stayed with her, she always invited her friends over. I'd gone to conferences with Mom, too—back when she worked as a patient advocate for a drug company—and everyone who's ever gone to a business conference knows there aren't exactly many kids there. I even had what some people considered "old person interests" like listening to seventies music (especially Billy Joel) and watching *The Golden Girls*, *The Young and the Restless*, and game shows like *Jeopardy!*. (Yes, my parents made fun of me for this!)

Talking to Alter felt different from talking to my friends in so many ways. We weren't shouting at each other over screaming kids at recess or whispering the latest gossip while we stretched next to each other in dance. We didn't have to cut our conversations short because our parents had just pulled up in front of school to pick us up, and we weren't begging our moms to let us use their phones so we could talk for five minutes before dinner. With Alter, there was *no rush*. We sat down, drank smoothies, and talked and talked.

"I receive dozens of emails every day," Alter had told me. "And I always take at least five minutes to write back the same day. My stepmother taught me that if someone took the time to write you, you owe them the same courtesy."

That's why I wasn't surprised when he wrote back to me only a few hours after I'd pressed *send*.

Date: June 1, 2014, 7:37 PM
From: Alter Wiener
To: Claire Sarnowski

Good evening Claire,

I am glad to hear from you. I felt
privileged to meet such a young girl with
such a mature mind.

I am sure that you are going to read my book from cover to cover and then give me your opinion or even better post your opinion on Amazon.com.

I don't write much because I don't have much free time; I don't even have time to die :)

Love to you,
Alter Wiener

Alter must have forgotten that I'd already read his book, but I *hadn't* reviewed it on Amazon. So I immediately opened Amazon's home page and typed in the words *From a Name to a Number* in the search bar. The cover popped up on the left-hand side of the page, featuring a photo of Alter's dark, haunted eyes and sunken face. When I'd visited his apartment, he'd told me this picture of him was taken right after the Russian army liberated him from his last camp, Waldenburg.

"Those of us who were prisoners learned a bit of each other's languages," he'd said. "So, I could understand some Russian. When I was freed, a Russian soldier approached me and said I should run free and kill, injure, or steal from any German soldier I met."

"Why didn't you?" I asked, without really thinking. Then I mentally kicked myself. Alter had been clear he didn't want revenge against *anyone*—even the people who had killed his family.

"Oh, I thought about it," he said as he straightened his jacket and tie, which I suddenly realized he hadn't taken off even though he was sitting in his own kitchen—wearing slippers, no less. "I wasn't the mature, sophisticated man you see before you now." He smiled. "I am joking. I was too weak to do anything like that."

Alter and I wrote back and forth, and a couple weeks later, my mom and I found ourselves driving the twenty miles from our house in Lake Oswego to Alter's apartment in Hillsboro. After we parked and approached his building, I realized I didn't know which door was his and started to panic.

Then I spied the pink mat.

"Mom, this is it!" I yelled.

"Come in, Claire and Carol, come in!" Alter said

when he opened the door, almost bouncing. "I have a surprise for you."

I'd been talking my mom's ear off the whole ride up and had of course told her about the smoothies Alter made the first time I'd visited. (Later, when I asked him what he put in the smoothies that made them so good, he said, "I always add love.") When we sat down at the small square table facing Alter's shelf, which I already affectionately thought of as his "Wall of Fame," I fully expected that his surprise was to make us another smoothie. Then I smelled the most wonderful smell coming out of the kitchen—like a combination of chicken soup and baked bread—and I knew I was in for something different.

"Would you like a bowl of my special matzo ball soup?" Alter asked.

I looked at my mom, confused. *Matzo ball soup?* I thought. *What's that?*

My mom nodded slightly, as if to assure me I'd like it.

"Um, yes, please," I said, trying not to seem clueless. "That sounds great."

In his slippers, Alter stepped into his small kitchen,

then emerged with three steaming bowls of soup on a tray.

After he set them in front of us, I looked down at the golden broth and noticed two meatball-sized lumps floating in it. They definitely weren't meatballs, so I assumed they must be matzo balls.

"Alter?" I said quietly. "I'm a little embarrassed to ask this, but what is matzo?"

Alter smiled kindly and didn't laugh. Instead, in the same even and courteous tone he'd used while recounting his experiences in the Holocaust to a few hundred wide-eyed middle schoolers, he explained it to me.

"Matzo is an unleavened bread that's part of the Jewish tradition. *Unleavened* means it's made without yeast, so it doesn't rise. The legend goes that the ancient Israelites who were enslaved in Egypt thousands of years ago didn't have time to wait for their bread to rise when they fled. So, to honor them, we eat unleavened bread at Passover. It is sort of like a cracker, and you can use it to make matzo balls to put in broth. Many cook with chicken broth, but I don't eat meat, so I use vegetable broth."

I dipped my spoon in and cut the matzo ball in half. It was spongey and light. Then I raised the spoon and sipped the broth, letting the matzo ball slide to the back of my mouth. It was *delicious*.

I was raised Catholic and went to a Christian preschool, and while I had some Jewish friends from school and dance classes, I didn't know much about Jewish culture. I was embarrassed about what I clearly hadn't learned, but part of me realized I'd grown up in a bubble. In Lake Oswego, most people identified as Christian. In elementary school, we didn't learn what the Jewish holidays were except for Hanukkah, and that was only because it was close to Christmas.

So why would Alter move from New York City—a place that, I knew from reading his book, welcomed thousands and thousands of Holocaust survivors after World War II—to somewhere like Hillsboro, Oregon? In fact, Alter had said in his speech he was one of the only Holocaust survivors alive in the whole state!

"When did you come to Oregon?" Mom asked between spoonfuls of soup.

"I moved from Forest Hills, Queens—in New York City—in 2000," he answered. "One of my two sons lived here, and he wanted my wife and me close by so we could have a quieter, easier life."

"Oh! I didn't know you had family around here," Mom said.

This is when we learned that Alter's wife, Esther, had aggressive Parkinson's disease and lived in a facility in New York—near one of their sons—that could take better care of her than Alter could. He said he had a hard time seeing her suffer, which is probably why he hadn't yet talked about her.

"It was not my plan to move to Oregon," Alter explained. "My wife and son wanted it. But it was the best thing that has ever happened to me. I have a new life here, with so many friends. I am making new memories every day."

Alter then told us about how when he first moved to Oregon, a fellow survivor encouraged him to join the Oregon Holocaust Resource Center. They have a speakers bureau that organizes speeches in Oregon and Washington.

"I gave my first speech in December 2000, at a local high school...," he said.

"I bet it was great!" I exclaimed.

"Well, not really," Alter answered. "I am not a natural speaker. My accent is thick, my vocabulary is limited, and...what high school student wants to sit and listen to an old man for an hour?"

I smiled and thought about how wrong he was about that.

"But apparently the students liked me. In fact, a year later, one of them—a girl—approached me at a store and said she'd decided not to drop out of school because of my speech. She felt terrible that I hadn't been allowed to have an education, so she decided to value hers."

I smiled even bigger. "Oh, that's wonderful, Alter."

"I keep up with some of the teachers and principals I meet at schools," he added. "These conversations turn into friendships, and I am always inviting people to come over to sit and talk—like now."

I'd just finished my soup, and I folded up my napkin carefully and placed it on the table. "So...," I asked tentatively. "Does that mean Mom and I might be able to...umm...see you again?" I didn't want to be pushy, but I had never met anyone like Alter before. I wanted to sit and talk with him as much as I could.

Alter didn't even pause. "Absolutely. You are welcome in my home anytime."

It took me a few days to work up the courage to contact Alter again, even though he had made it clear I could come back to visit.

Alter didn't have a cell phone, so texting was not an option. Because his hearing was declining, he didn't like using the phone, either. So, email it was. I wrote him, he wrote back, and before I knew it, Mom and I were going to Hillsboro to visit him once every month or six weeks.

My mom usually asked Alter if he needed help with anything and he always told us that he would never ask us to run an errand or go to an appointment with him.

"My time is for *you*, not for crossing things off my to-do list," he said one day.

He was always true to his word.

"You are precious," Alter also loved to say. Then he'd stand up, adjust his suspenders, and smooth out his shirt and pants so they weren't wrinkled. "Tell me what you're reading now. Anything good?"

I was going through a huge historical fiction phase, so I told him about a novel I'd picked up called *The Watsons Go to Birmingham — 1963*.

"It's so good, Alter. It takes place in 1963 and is all about a Black family's experience during the Civil Rights Movement."

"Ah, yes," Alter said, nodding his head. "When I moved to America in 1960, it was a great relief to see Black people standing up for their rights and fighting oppression because I didn't have that chance as a young man. Sadly, there is still so much work to do here in America...." He paused. "I bet you haven't learned much about the Civil Rights Movement in school, have you?"

I had to think for a moment. "No...," I answered slowly. "I mean, they taught us about Martin Luther King Jr. in kindergarten, and we celebrate Black History Month every February." I paused again. "*Celebrate* is probably more than we actually do. It's more like we touch on it, if that makes sense. We read books about Rosa Parks and Martin Luther King Jr. from the Who Was? series, and once I had to write a short essay about a famous Black person in history, but that was it. I guess I haven't learned much else about the Civil Rights Movement because...maybe...I'm still in elementary school...?"

Alter cut me off. "That shouldn't matter. You are never too young to learn about justice and what's wrong and right. You are never too young to be taught about human history."

That was just what Mom had said when she'd told me about the Holocaust.

I thought about school and what we focused on. We spent so much time learning things like fractions and how settlers in wagons rolled along the Oregon Trail toward the sea in the mid-1800s, but almost everything I knew about the Civil Rights Movement was from *The Watsons Go to Birmingham – 1963*. Why *weren't* we taught about civil rights? For that matter, why weren't we taught about the Holocaust?

"Alter?" I asked, changing the subject. "What have you been reading?"

In response, Alter moved toward his desk and picked something up from it.

"Carol, Claire, I want you to see this."

Alter handed Mom a three-page, single-spaced

document with a headline at the top. As Mom scanned the page, her eyes grew wide.

"These are all the books you've read *this year?*" she asked.

"Yes," he answered. "I've been busy. Just like Claire, I read everything I can get my hands on."

Alter then motioned to a bookshelf next to the couch. "There's my Scrabble board. I've been playing most of my life. I learned a lot of English through Scrabble."

Mom looked shocked. "But half the words in the Scrabble dictionary are words you'd never use in real life!"

Alter smiled. "I like to be mysterious."

I had just taken a sip of my matzo ball soup, and I almost snorted it out of my nose.

"I know, it's funny," Alter continued, "but Scrabble has meant a lot to me. I have Scrabble dates with friends almost every week. And if I meet someone new and they have a hard time opening up, I always play Scrabble with them. It helps us connect."

Who would have a hard time opening up to Alter? I wondered. He was easier to talk to than almost anyone I'd met in my life.

Alter settled back down into the seat next to me. "Reading is vital to understanding our history, but I want to know what's happening in the world around me, too. So every morning after I wake up, I walk to New Seasons Market, just down the road. I buy a newspaper there."

"Why don't you have the paper delivered?" I asked. "Or better yet, read it online?"

He looked at me like I had three heads. "Claire, you still have a lot to learn about old people and their relationships with computers."

I smiled, thinking about how sometimes my grandma couldn't even figure out how to use her cell phone. Then, right on cue, Alter's computer chirped with a sound I'd heard every time I'd visited him.

"You've got mail!"

That's right. Alter still used AOL.

"I once got the newspaper delivered," he said, "but it came too late. I hate when things are late. But the real reason I go to New Seasons is because I like meeting new people."

Alter went on to explain that the staff at New Seasons knew him so well that some had become friends.

The same thing happened with the customers there, too. In fact, he said that a few months earlier he'd met a group of Jehovah's Witnesses there.

"One of the women in the group recognized me from a speech I had given. She called me over and invited me to sit with her and her group and have coffee. I pulled up a chair and made some new friends."

"Have you seen them since?" I asked, knowing he liked having people over.

"Oh, yes, I've had them over for lunch a couple times. I hold a very special place in my heart for the Jehovah's Witnesses because I was in Blechhammer with a group of them."

I hadn't even realized non-Jews had also been persecuted during the Holocaust.

"They were forced to wear purple triangles, so they were easy to recognize," Alter explained. "They told me that their church organization had always opposed war, so they refused to join the Nazi party. They wouldn't let their children be in the Hitler Youth, they refused military service, and they wouldn't give the Nazi salute or fly the Nazi flag. So the Nazis sent about three thousand Jehovah's Witnesses into concentration camps."

Alter paused, then continued. "I learned so much from the Jehovah's Witnesses at Blechhammer. Even though we came from different places and had different backgrounds, we were bound by our experiences. We were linked by our refusal to be bitter. We knew that hate and resentment weren't going to get us out of the camps, and anger wasn't going to keep us alive. Instead, we needed hope, faith, and a vision for a better future, and we shared that in the few moments we could speak every day."

"I'm not sure I'd be able to be so optimistic if my life had been stolen from me," I responded.

"You'd be surprised, Claire," Alter said kindly. "Sometimes you're just too tired to feel hate. So you choose hope instead."

"Mom?" I asked as we got back into her car to head home. "When are we seeing Aunt Sue?"

"Why, honey?"

I couldn't shake the thought that there were giant holes in my education. I had this sinking feeling that there were so many things I *wasn't* learning in school and could learn only from books or from people like Alter, who were sticking their necks out trying to make the past seem real.

"I want to ask her about why she teaches what she does, or why I haven't learned much about civil rights...I mean, beyond the basic facts about Martin Luther King Jr....or about the Holocaust. Maybe these are things we're going to learn later in school. But maybe not...?"

"We can call her anytime," Mom answered as she started the car. "I like the questions you're asking."

CHAPTER FIVE

✦

FACE THE PAST

ONE OF THE NEXT TIMES I SAW ALTER'S PRESENTATION, I was in fifth grade, and it was at my own elementary school, River Grove. I was on top of the world because it had been my idea to invite him, and I was going to help him with his slideshow! For weeks leading up to the day, it was all I could talk about. I couldn't wait for people to hear Alter.

Aunt Sue had confirmed that a lot of her students were completely in the dark about the Holocaust. "In fact," she told me, "that's one of the reasons I wanted Alter to come to my school. Unless one of their teachers decides to work the Holocaust into a lesson or reading list—or unless they meet someone like Alter—students might get to high school or even college without ever learning about it."

I was hoping Alter could prevent that from happening at *my* school.

Luckily, River Grove's principal agreed. "This will be an excellent learning experience for our students!" he said.

The day of Alter's speech, I was so excited I could hardly stand it. At school, I'd told everyone who'd listen about how important Alter's speech was going to be, and I could tell Mom and Dad just wanted the day to end so I would finally talk about something else at the dinner table. (I'm kidding. Sort of.)

I'd given my principal a printed copy of Alter's PowerPoint presentation because he wanted to look it over and know what to expect. This wasn't unusual; Alter said he frequently showed teachers or administrators his slides beforehand. But what *was* unusual was what my principal said to me about an hour before Alter arrived.

"Claire," he said as a serious look crossed his face. "I need you to remove slides twenty-two and twenty-five."

I didn't remember what those slides were, so I

flipped through the packet and found them. They featured two black-and-white photos of Jewish prisoners digging mass graves. You could see a pile of shrouded bodies on one side of the photos, but those images definitely weren't graphic. You couldn't see faces or features of the dead people; that wasn't the point of this picture. It was the *act* of innocent people digging graves for their friends and neighbors that packed the emotional punch. Alter talked about how that happened a lot, but this image helped make it more real. It was similar to how I'd felt when I first saw the slides of his grandmother and father. These were *human beings* who'd been killed, not some page in a history textbook.

"But—" I stammered, afraid to contradict him. He *was* the principal, after all. "Alter has given this same presentation to third and fourth graders, and it wasn't a problem *then*. I saw the slides for the first time when *I* was in fourth grade. Besides, he only shows these slides for a few seconds, and it's hard to make anything out. Are you...sure we can't include them?"

My principal just shook his head, and I knew better than to push it.

Alter used to worry about describing the more traumatizing events he'd endured to kids my age and younger. But then an elementary school teacher whose class he was preparing to speak to told him he shouldn't be concerned. She felt that this kind of knowledge, although upsetting, was essential to help young people grow.

"Today's kids watch television and are familiar with violent scenes," she said. "They have to learn about the Holocaust and listen to the personal experience of Holocaust victims as long as they are alive."

I hadn't thought about it before, but she was right. Never mind what's on TV or social media; most of the kids at my school had read a *lot* of scary stuff, from *Wings of Fire* to *Where the Red Fern Grows* to *The Hunger Games*. Sure, these books are fiction, and some of these stories frightened me a little (I can admit that now!), but they were teaching me bravery and how to wrap my brain around uncomfortable ideas.

Alter's story had done the same thing. But—unlike the characters in those books—he was real, and he made me think about the world beyond my family, friends, and community. I really hoped my classmates would feel something similar. If Alter made the same impression on them that he'd made on me, his sometimes upsetting stories would help them grow into middle schoolers who would be able to cope with reality, not hide from it. His message of hope would help them embrace others, not create divisions.

An hour later, when I saw my mom walk in with Alter and lead him up the stage to the spot where he was set to speak, my excitement had turned into anxiety.

I'm not going to have time to tell him about the missing slides before his speech begins.

Then I wiped the worried expression off my face and tried to convince myself that it would all be fine.

"Hello, everyone," my fifth-grade teacher, Mr. McCarroll, said into the microphone. "I would like to introduce everyone to our distinguished guest and speaker, Alter Wiener."

And then there was Alter, giving his presentation: sharing his experiences, his belief in the importance of education, and his vision that the world could come together and better itself not through grief and anger, but through hope and healing divisions. He talked about the people he'd lost, too: His strict and religious father, who prayed three times a day, worked long hours at the grocery below their apartment to provide for his family, and every Saturday asked Alter to give him a full account of his studies. Then his older brother, Schmuel, who was ripped away from their home by the Nazis in the dead of night in June 1941 and taken to a slave labor camp. His half brother, Hirsh, eight years younger than him, whom he'd last seen crying and clinging to his stepmom's apron while Alter was dragged away from home and taken to the camps. In February 1943, when Hirsh was nine, the Nazis deported him and his mom to Auschwitz, and he was killed in the gas chambers soon after his arrival.

"Every time I get in the shower," Alter said. "I look up at the showerhead and imagine poison gas coming out from it. I am horrified to think of the pain my poor brother endured in his last moments. He was just a child."

Alter moved from one slide to another, describing each. He talked about slide twenty, then twenty-one. Each was small and grainy, and he allowed his words to explain what the crowd's eyes couldn't see. When he got to what should have been slide twenty-two, he paused and turned to me.

"Claire," he whispered, "There seems to be a slide missing."

I cringed.

He moved on to slides twenty-three and twenty-four. When he got to twenty-five, his forehead wrinkled up when he realized it was missing, too.

"Where is my slide?" he asked in a whisper.

"I...I'll explain," I muttered. "Afterward."

I hated that I had caused him to pause in the middle of his presentation when the crowd was sitting at the edge of their seats. Deep down, though, I suspected something so minor wouldn't stop him. He'd been through so much, and he always forged ahead, determined and optimistic. That was Alter's way.

Soon he began to talk about the mothers in his life. His own mother, Pearl, died of a heart condition when he was four years old. He didn't remember her face or the lullabies she sang to him when he was a baby, but he did recall the day his family's maid picked him up from school and told him that his mom was gone. His father remarried the following year, to a woman named Rachel, and she was kind, compassionate, and raised Schmuel and Alter like her own. She, too, was killed at Auschwitz. Alter didn't know she'd died until after he was freed from the camps when he was eighteen.

While Alter spoke about his family, I looked around at the audience. Toward the back of the room, I noticed a girl was wiping her eyes.

I know, this is so hard to hear, I thought. Then I remembered: Her mom had died from brain cancer that year. If Alter could make it through losing two mothers *and* his whole family, maybe she'd learned she could, too.

My mind flashed back to the missing slides. *Nobody can remove anyone's pain by hiding the truth,* I thought. By facing even the most painful facts, I knew we could learn, grow, and move forward—no matter how young we were.

CHAPTER SIX

✦

CAN WE DO MORE?

MIDDLE SCHOOL FEELS LIKE A BIG LEAP—MORE homework, more tests, and (*gasp!*) receiving grades for *everything*. I'd always tried to study hard and do my best at school, though, so I was actually looking forward to sixth grade. What I wasn't happy about was missing my favorite after-school activities. I'd broken my ankle recently (for the second time!), so dance classes and competitions were on hold indefinitely. Nor could I play soccer, a sport I'd fallen in love with.

Luckily, life quickly settled into a new, comforting rhythm, and that was thanks to Alter. Without dance and soccer, I could visit him almost every weekend. I had so much fun sharing everything with him, from my new interest in photography to the One Direction concert I'd gone to that summer with Aunt Sue (it was the best night of my life—and still is!).

Alter shared everything with me, too.

"I took a day trip to Powell's the other day with a group of survivors I see once a month," Alter said to me on one crisp early fall weekend when we decided to sit outside and talk. "That is my favorite bookstore. By the way...who is One Direction?"

"Oh, my gosh, Alter, they're this band from England, but one of the lead singers is Irish. It's five guys, and..." Then I stopped myself.

How could I explain the magic of Harry Styles to Alter?

"I'm waiting, Claire," Alter said, starting to laugh. Then his face turned positively wistful. "I enjoy talking to you about things you like. My son always told me I dwelled too much on the Holocaust. I think it made him feel I wasn't interested in *him*."

I knew Alter and his sons didn't see each other very often, and he'd said a few times how painful that was to him.

"I'm sorry, Alter," I finally said, struggling with the

fact that I was suddenly in the strange position of comforting someone nine times my age.

"It's all right," he answered, then looked up to the trees that lined the parking lot outside his apartment complex. "I wasn't always the best father, but I hope my sons realize I struggled because of my trauma. I love them very much." He sighed ever so slightly, and his gaze shifted from the trees to me. "And I love this time with you on this beautiful day. Now, tell me, how is school?"

I wanted to connect with Alter about his sons, but it was hard. I *was* only eleven. "It's really good," I answered, relieved to change the subject. "I've made a bunch of new friends already. One of them is this girl named Hannah. We have so much in common, Alter."

Alter didn't seem very excited for me, which was odd. "Are these friends nice to you?" he asked, searching my face in a way that made me a little suspicious.

"Um, yes. . . . Why do you ask?"

"Middle school can be difficult," Alter answered. "I have spoken to many middle schools over the years, and I know there is a lot of bullying at that age—usually more than in elementary school. Groups of friends form and change, and some people simply become *mean*."

I thought back to my first year at River Grove Elementary, which was my third-grade year. I'd gone to another school—Bryant Elementary—before that, but the Lake Oswego School Board had closed Bryant down, so I'd had to switch schools. Even though dozens of other Bryant kids transferred with me, some River Grove students treated us like we didn't belong. They didn't want us to sit with them at lunch. They stared at us when we walked down the halls.

"Kids *can* be really mean sometimes," I finally said to Alter. "But I'm okay. I promise."

Alter cleared his throat and smiled. "If anyone gives you any trouble at this new school, they will have to face me." Then he balled up his fists and flexed his biceps.

Most of my classmates were taller than Alter, so I just laughed and shook my head. "Oh, Alter." I sighed. "I'll be fine."

A few months later, Mom and I arrived at Alter's apartment, just like we did almost every weekend. Instead of being excited, though, I was an absolute mess.

"The most upsetting this happened this week, Alter,"

I said as he placed three smoothies on the table and sat down. He situated himself in his chair, crossed his legs, and waited for me to go on. "I don't know if you know what Instagram is...."

Alter looked at me blankly. So, I took a deep breath and described the social media site.

"Anyway, a girl I know had to leave school because she was being bullied so badly on Instagram. Well, she didn't *have* to leave. She chose to. Being in school and seeing all the people who were so mean to her was just too painful for her."

"I'm confused," Alter said after a pause. "How was she being bullied?"

"Oh, sorry," I replied, realizing he couldn't visualize how Instagram works. "A few people created fake usernames on Instagram and used them to make fun of her. They posted horrible things in the comment section under her photos."

Alter became very still, as if he was thinking hard. "Why would you do something like that?" He uncrossed his legs, then took off his glasses and clutched them in one hand. "Why would you hide behind a false identity in order to inflict cruelty on another person?"

"I'm not sure," I answered honestly. "It seems so cowardly. If you have something you want to say to someone, tell them to their face."

"Though you should be kind," Alter added.

"I guess?" I said, not sure where he was going with this. I looked over at Mom, and she nodded her head, like she wanted me to continue. "Anyhow, my friends and I have been trying to help her. She has no idea why this is happening because she didn't do *anything*. And now she doesn't want to come back to school."

I gazed across the table and noticed Alter staring straight ahead. I could tell he was thinking about something, but I knew it might take him a while to get it out. He didn't want his words to be hasty. He wanted them to be just right.

"Whoever bullied your friend probably just wants to feel powerful," he said slowly. "They are in a weak place in their lives, and that act made them feel strong."

"I guess I can see that," I said with a sigh, "but it still makes me angry."

Alter smiled. "Of course you're angry. That's natural. But you don't have to react immediately. Take some time to process your anger, and then figure out what to do with it. Youth is the best time to learn to be better, not bitter. Even on...Instag...what is it?"

"Instagram." I tried to stifle a giggle. Then—timed just right—his computer rang out. "You've got mail!"

"In-sta-gram," Alter responded, stretching out each syllable and waving his long, slender fingers as if he was swatting away a mosquito. "Whatever it is. Keep true to the high values you hold in your heart. You can move on from anger and resentment."

Then Alter reminded me of a story he'd written about in his book. In February 1943, he was standing in line with a fellow concentration camp prisoner, and the two struck up a conversation. They weren't breaking any stated rule by talking, but a guard approached them with a look of rage on his face. The guard grabbed Alter's hand, pressed a lit cigarette into his palm, punched him in the mouth, and growled at him.

"Cursed Jew, you will never be able to talk again."

Alter began bleeding, then spit out a few of his teeth.

As Alter was feeling around his bleeding mouth to see which teeth he still had, he noticed that the ones that hadn't fallen out were leaning at an odd angle.

Then he looked up and saw the German guard clutching his hand.

"He had injured his hand when he hit me," Alter recounted. "Like so many bullies, he didn't think twice about hurting me, but he couldn't stand to be hurt himself."

"Alter...?" I asked, my voice rising higher by a few notes. "If bullies don't care about other people's pain, why should I forgive them?"

"Because when you remain resentful or bitter for a long time, you poison yourself," he answered. "It's better to *learn* from the past, or *understand* the bad things done to you, so that you can do the opposite in the future."

Once again, Mom's words about her experience visiting Dachau echoed in my head. "When we forget about history, Claire," she had said, "we're doomed to repeat it."

"It took me time," Alter said confidently, "but now I know that if I had remained bitter about losing my teeth, or my family...or...everything I'd ever known and loved, I'd have nothing *but* bitterness. What happened to me in the past motivates me to teach others so *they* can be better in the future."

I paused, still frustrated. "Alter, you make it sound so logical, but I just don't think kids my age are thinking about much beyond their friends and homework and Instagram...remember Instagram?" I giggled, then got serious again. "I mean, your speeches are incredible, but you're only one person. Shouldn't *everyone* my age learn the lessons you've taught me?"

Alter reached out his hands and patted mine. Suddenly, I realized he didn't look all that confident anymore. "Yes, Claire. But I'm an old man. I have tried to enlist the help of politicians and educators to make sure our schools teach all students about the Holocaust, but I have never had luck. I sometimes feel alone in my work. Luckily, though, that work has allowed me to make friends like you."

Mom piped up. "What do you mean, you've tried to work with politicians before?"

Alter looked down, and I could tell he was getting tired. "Don't worry about it now. I will tell you when we have more time. I don't want the subject to wear me out." He sighed. He really *was* tired.

We talked for a few more minutes—about my ankle (it was healing!) and the trip Hannah and I had made to the mall, then about what I was hoping to get for Christmas. Alter talked a little about some of the speeches he had coming up in the next few months, and then he mentioned the fact that his granddaughter and great-grandson were soon coming to visit. He couldn't wait to see them.

"Alter," I said, suddenly feeling something spark inside me. It was the same fire that had started when I first heard Alter speak at Aunt Sue's school. "If it's okay with you, I want to talk more about Holocaust education later on. I just feel like...like...I can do something more. Maybe?"

"I would like that, Claire."

CHAPTER SEVEN

WHY DOES ANYONE THINK IT'S OKAY?

BY THE FALL OF 2016, I WAS IN SEVENTH GRADE and had been visiting Alter at least three or four times every month. I even helped him at some of his speeches, carrying books, showing him where to sign them for people, and running his slide presentations.

Our conversations had long since settled into a rhythm. My mom and I would walk into his apartment, give Alter a hug, and sit down at his square table. Alter would ask us what we'd like in our smoothies, then he'd shuffle off to the kitchen to make them. As the blender whirred in his small kitchen, we'd pick up a chocolate or a cracker from the spread he'd laid out on the table, and a minute or so later, my mom would help Alter carry the smoothies from the kitchen. As we sipped them, we'd talk about all the things we'd done or read or seen that week. Words flowed from one subject to the next without any awkward transitions, long pauses, or moments spent wondering when you'd get a word in edgewise. Inevitably, the conversation would move into current events, and while sometimes we were happy about what was going on in the world, sometimes one of us was troubled.

About four or five times every hour his computer would break through the conversation, chiming, "You've got mail!" I'd start to giggle, then try to refocus on whatever we'd been discussing. Laughing, crying, or reminiscing, Alter and I shared *everything*. He was home for me. He was starting to become my world.

One day, Alter announced he'd been thinking about something. He was ninety years old, and he said he realized it was time to retire from his speeches. His mind was as sharp as ever, but his voice was thinner, he stood less often, and when he was on his feet, he moved more slowly and unsteadily.

"Are you sure?" I asked hesitantly.

———————•———————

"Yes, I'm sure," he answered, with a sad but determined tone in his voice.

Alter was right, but I hated that so many people were going to miss hearing him talk. I hated that he was getting frailer by the day. But I guess it was all part of the progression of time. We'd both grown older, and our lives had changed.

The world had started to change, too.

2016 was a presidential election year, and Donald Trump was facing off against Hillary Clinton in one of the most controversial, tense, and divisive races in American history. In fact, the political climate was *anything* but peaceful. Half the country seemed to be horrified by what they saw as Trump's intolerance and bullying, and the other half was thrilled that the reality star turned unlikely presidential candidate wasn't afraid to speak his mind. The melting pot America was supposed to be had boiled over, and racial and ethnic tensions had grown sky-high all around the country.

"I became an American citizen in 1966, when I was forty years old," Alter said a few weeks before the election. "I have voted in every single election after that, and I am grateful every time."

"But this election is pretty tense," I answered. I was still six years away from being able to vote, but I'd always paid attention to every election, big or small. I even read the voters' guide we always received in the mail—cover to cover. "Alter, are you worried? Mom, Dad, and I see reports of hate crimes on the news every single week, and I can't be on social media without witnessing someone get into a *huge* political fight." I paused. "I just feel like we're starting to see the hateful side of people."

Alter remained silent. His face darkened, and then he rubbed his eyes. His computer chirped again. "You've got mail!"

This time, I didn't laugh.

Not long after, I was doing homework on our living room couch while my mom made dinner in the kitchen. She was watching the Portland nightly news—something she turned on almost every night—and my dad was sitting near me, looking at his phone. The volume was low enough that it didn't bother me but high enough that I could hear what the news anchors were reporting.

Suddenly, I heard them say the words "Lake Oswego High School." Mom did, too.

"Ken! Claire!" she called toward me and Dad. "I think they're about to say something important!"

I ran to the TV, and my dad put down his phone and followed close behind me. As the three of us stared at the television, our jaws dropped.

The news anchor and on-air correspondent reported that at the end of October, someone had posted something disturbing on the unofficial Lake Oswego High School class of 2017 Facebook page. In response to a poll asking for suggestions about what the senior prank should be, most people had written things like "coat the stairs with Vaseline" or "bring a dog to school." But someone else suggested this:

"Create a club called Ku-Klux-Klub and find every Black kid and sacrifice them."

For days, that post sat there on the page. No one challenged it. No one called it out. No one asked the page administrator to take it down or block the user, and no one reported it to teachers or school administrators. Day after day, people saw the post and didn't express outrage or seek justice against the person who'd written it. They just plain ignored it, and it wasn't until early November that someone finally told the Lake Oswego High School administration about it.

"What is *wrong* with people?" I asked Mom and Dad in disbelief.

"I'm just as shocked that no one did anything to stop it as I am at the post!" Dad said.

"I know," I answered. "But times are really stressful right now, and so many people are *angry*. I guess I shouldn't be surprised."

Unfortunately, this felt like *more* than anger.

Over dinner that night, Mom, Dad, and I couldn't stop talking about why the Facebook incident had happened.

"I think people ignored the post because it didn't seem like a big deal to them," I said. "They haven't been educated about why posting something like that is so wrong, and they also don't understand that what they write is bad enough to *hurt* another person."

Mom nodded her head. "I think you nailed it."

"I mean, I know it's not the same, but remember how I changed the way I talk after I met Alter? I used to say, 'I'm starving!' when I was hungry. Now I understand the power of those words. Alter starved and almost died. I've skipped *maybe* two meals in my life."

As I picked at my dinner, something hit me. My mom and dad embarrassed me or seemed uncool sometimes (ahem, I *was* a preteen), but I was lucky they'd raised me to be open-minded and sensitive and told me to take a stand against any forms of hate I saw in the world. Even when I rolled my eyes at them or wished I was on my phone texting my friends instead of watching the news with them, I was grateful they engaged me in politics and current events.

Sometimes, that awareness was something I really needed in Lake Oswego.

Unless you're from Oregon—or maybe the Pacific Northwest—you're probably unfamiliar with my normally sleepy hometown.

Lake Oswego is a quiet, upper-middle-class Portland suburb that wraps around Oswego Lake, a deep motorboat lake just to the west of the Willamette River. Tall Douglas firs span the lakeshore, cute small businesses dot downtown, and sculptures line A Avenue, one of the main thoroughfares. There are a school and tennis courts just down the street from my house, and in my neighborhood, kids trick or treat without their parents. We have a weekly farmers market, a Fourth of July parade, summer concerts, and a Tinseltown Trolley that Santa and Mrs. Claus ride on every Christmas season. People in Lake Oswego often don't lock up their houses or cars, and if they aren't working at home, you can find a lot of them commuting back and forth to Intel or Nike, two of Portland's biggest employers.

Even though there have been a few small populations of Asian Americans, Indian Americans, and Latinx people on the south side of the lake (where my house is) for as long as I've been alive, Lake Oswego has been about 85 percent white. Portland is seen as pretty liberal, but our community still wasn't very progressive sometimes. I knew people who denied the existence of racism or classism, and many said or did intolerant things because no one they knew would be directly affected by their actions.

I didn't think that the majority of people in Lake Oswego believed that other races, religions, or ethnic groups were inferior to them, but I worried a lot of them didn't *notice* the issue. Maybe racism didn't affect them. Maybe antisemitism and hate speech hadn't been directed at them. Unlike Alter, a system of intolerance and oppression hadn't shaped who they are.

Thinking about this at dinner that night, I felt ill. The kids in the Lake Oswego class of 2017 Facebook group hadn't spoken out about the racist Facebook post because it seemed far away from the Friday night football game, the Tinseltown Trolley, and the boats dotting our majestic lake. But the sad truth was that prejudice—and in particular racism—was *everywhere.*

And right now it was in my backyard.

When I went to bed that night, I couldn't stop thinking about a story Alter had told me.

"My last concentration camp was called Waldenburg," he'd said. "It was in what's now western Poland but was at the time Germany. The area was desolate, with no trees anywhere...." Alter had gestured wildly with both hands, as if he were sweeping away any vegetation or trace of life. He had a way of telling stories that brought a scene vividly alive—even if that scene was one of utter destruction.

Alter placed his hands on his lap and continued. "When the Russian army liberated the camp, the prisoners had no idea where to go or what to do. We had been locked away for so long that we were in shock, unable to think or act. I decided to stay where I was and rummage through the camp's pantry for food."

"Was there anything there?" I'd interrupted.

"Not much," he'd answered. "Some raw potatoes, which I gladly ate."

I'd thought about the bitter taste of a raw potato and made a face.

"That day, several German women from the nearby town showed up carrying some items. I had no idea people lived close by. I hadn't seen a single woman or child the entire time I was there...."

My heart felt heavy. Alter must have been *so* lonely.

"One of the women walked up to me and offered me a dish of food and a shaggy beige sweater. Then she burst into tears."

"Did she say anything?" I'd asked, always eager for all the details Alter could offer, even if they made my heart ache. "Did she apologize?"

"I don't remember if she apologized," Alter had answered, "but that's not what I was looking for. I was too tired to be upset. Instead, she said that everyone knew there was a labor camp in the vicinity but that they had no idea that the prisoners were so badly mistreated. I believe her words were, 'I was blinded for so long, but now I see the horror!' "

Coming back to the present, I rolled onto my side, then shifted to my other side. *If only kids in Lake Oswego could see the effects of intolerance and hate, too*, I thought. *Maybe they'd change their actions.*

I drifted off into a fitful sleep that night, feeling like I was standing on the edge of something, but wondering where that was and what I could do.

On Election Day morning, I logged on to my computer like I always did after I woke up. Instead of a few emails from friends or Alter, though, I was surprised to see something marked "urgent" from our superintendent. In her email, she attached a message from the principal of Lake Oswego High School, Rollin Dickinson. Mr. Dickinson started by mentioning the Facebook posts, then he referenced something else.

It was so shocking it made my stomach twist and turn into knots.

Apparently, on the day before Yom Kippur a few weeks earlier (Yom Kippur is one of the holiest days in Judaism), someone taped up an antisemitic image in the LOHS cafeteria. It was a photo printout of a concentration camp prisoner being pushed into an oven, and underneath it was a caption that read "Easy-Bake Oven." An administrator had discovered this after he saw a student taking a photo of the picture with his phone. When he realized what it was, the administrator tore it down immediately.

What? I thought. *Someone had posted an antisemitic poster in the LOHS cafeteria?!* Then I realized something. Once again, a student stood by and watched this disgusting, horrible, unethical, deeply harmful post just *remain there* without doing anything. This person didn't rip it up and throw it in the trash. They didn't run as fast as they could to tell a teacher or the principal. They didn't pull out a sharpie and mark through the words or image. Nope. They reached for their phone and took a picture instead.

How could anyone think that was okay?

I had no clue, but there was one thing I felt certain of: If whoever put up that poster had known Alter's story, they wouldn't have done something like this.

"I don't understand any of this, Claire," Alter said to me and Mom that Saturday, worry creeping into his voice. "In my time, I lived through people being murdered because of who they are. Do children really believe and accept this kind of hate?"

"Not everyone," I said quickly, because I was so eager for him not to feel helpless. "My friends and I are really upset. This and the election are all we've talked about all week."

"I know, I know." He sighed. "That's what I keep telling myself. I've met many students your age who are kind and loving, and they give me hope. But it's hard not to feel discouraged, too."

I met Alter's eyes. Once again, I found myself in the strange position of trying to placate the worries of someone who'd lived a lifetime shaped by fear and loss. But instead of feeling uncomfortable about it this time, it seemed more natural. Alter was a rock for me. As I grew up, why couldn't I be the same for him?

"Something really encouraging happened the other day, Alter," I responded slowly. "Right after the 'Easy-Bake Oven' scandal, the staff of the Lake Oswego High School student newspaper dedicated an entire issue to the subject of racism. Right on the front page, they created a time line of all the racist incidents that have happened at the school over the last few years."

Alter cleared his throat uncomfortably.

"I know it sounds really sad, but they were making a point. Instead of forgetting these awful events or acting like they were just 'bad things that happened,' they *owned* what had gone down over the years. They held it under a microscope and acknowledged how terrible so many people had been."

"So, students aren't forgetting the past...," Alter said slowly.

"No," I answered. "They're using it to try to learn something and improve."

"Well, that is very good. Now, what is the school system doing, other than the emails to parents and the statements in the press?"

Mom looked at me like she wanted to answer this one, and I was fine with that. Her concerns were 100 percent in line with mine. "There's not been much, unfortunately. They said they had a seminar and a few class discussions, and some students made a pledge to 'Be Kind Online,' but I'm not sure that's enough. The school district hasn't really used these two incidents as an opportunity to bring people together in a *real* way, if that makes sense. I haven't heard of any programming changes or new classes, for example."

"Has anything been done at your middle school?" Alter asked me.

"Not really," I answered. "It's like the acts were discussed in the halls and by a few teachers, and we all condemned them. But then everyone moved on with their lives."

Which would be fine, I thought, *if students and the community had truly, fundamentally changed.*

We hadn't changed, but we were getting close. At least some of the time.

Early on the morning of March 1, 2017—five months after the "Easy-Bake Oven" incident—a few students discovered racist graffiti on the walls of three boys' bathrooms at Lake Oswego High School. These young people took pictures and then cleaned the graffiti from the walls. They also notified the school office right away, and the administration contacted the police and started their own internal investigation.

A week later, hundreds of LOHS students staged a walkout with the full backing of the school administration and the district, who promised not to penalize anyone for missing class that morning. As rain fell lightly on the crowd, students carried signs and a few class leaders gave speeches over a loudspeaker. News crews came to film, and from my desk across the lake at Lakeridge Middle School, I could even feel the impact. I started to sense that maybe, just maybe, the gravity of the issue was sinking in.

In language arts class that day, I was pretty sure we were about to finish up our discussions of *Roll of Thunder, Hear My Cry*, a classic novel about a Black family during the Depression who suffers racism and violence yet remains strong. The main character, a nine-year-old named Cassie Logan, had so much courage and pride, and she wasn't afraid to speak her mind or stand up for justice. Her personality and strength inspired me, and she felt like a combination of Anne

Frank and Hermione Granger rolled into one amazing package.

I loved my language arts teacher that year. She was smart and warm in every conversation she had with our class, and her discussions about everything from literature to current events always got me thinking. When I reached class and the bell rang, she walked to the front of the room with a somber look on her face.

"I have something I need to talk to everyone about," she said slowly as her voice started to crack. "I know a lot of you are aware of last week's incident at Lake Oswego High School." Then she paused for a few uncomfortable moments, and I think I saw tears forming in the corner of her eyes.

"Many students at Lake Oswego High School skipped class this morning to participate in a walkout," she said. "They stood outside, spoke against racism, and carried signs. The administration and district supported them, and I do, too. In fact, I think it's urgent that the students on this side of the lake also take a stand against the racist and antisemitic incidents that happened."

I noticed her voice had grown stronger, but suddenly,

she broke down in sobs. I felt my shoulders tense up as she walked to her desk to get a tissue, wiped her eyes, and returned to the front of class.

"None of you have ever seen me cry, so I'll explain why I am," she continued. "Last week a teacher here found similar graffiti on a classroom desk. Someone had drawn nooses. *Nooses.* I reported it to the principal, and the desk has been removed." Tears sprang back into her eyes, and she wiped them away. "We have been reading *Roll of Thunder, Hear My Cry,* which is a book about racism. About surviving violence and intolerance. About being a stronger person despite what people say or do to you." She sniffled and blew her nose. "The fact that a student didn't understand this...," my teacher continued. "The fact that a student chose to engage in a deliberate act of racist hate *in this school* is the saddest thing that has happened in my many years of teaching."

My heart was racing, and I could feel the heat rising in my face. This had happened in *my* school, by *my* classmates, in *my* grade.

I have to do something. I have to do something, I thought. That phrase pounded like rolling thunder inside me. In the twelve years of my life, I might have been little, and I might have been shy or nervous sometimes, but Mom and Dad had always taught me to *act*. I'd knocked on doors to raise money. I'd written letters. I'd walked (and sometimes strolled) in Walk MS. In elementary school, I'd brought Alter to my school to speak so he could open people's eyes. But more was needed. The intolerance had to stop, and it had to stop *now*.

Now.

I knew there was only one person who could help me figure out what to do: Alter.

CHAPTER EIGHT

✦

ACT NOW

"I DON'T KNOW WHO DID IT," I TOLD ALTER THAT weekend as I stabbed my spoon into a matzo ball. "But I'm sure it was someone I know."

His response was firm. "If you ever find out, I hope you are kind to them, Claire. Even people who do wrong deserve compassion. But I know you probably would be. I can't imagine you being unkind."

Alter always thought the best of me and knew I tried to make decisions with my heart *and* my head. Staying balanced was going to be harder this time than others, though. I was angrier than I'd been in my whole life.

"I will be kind," I insisted. "But I hope they

understand the harm they caused. I hope the school does *something* to show them that."

Alter lifted up both hands in parallel, gesturing firmly to make his point. "If the school chooses to punish this person, that is their business. But there must be healing. You and the rest of the school must be better, not bitter."

I smiled. Alter always had a way of making me feel calm. "You love that phrase," I said.

"Because it is the truth," Alter answered.

I couldn't let go of the urgent feeling I had in my gut that I needed to be doing more, though. I couldn't just wait for change; I had to *be* the change that happens. So I asked Alter the question that had been nagging at me since I first heard about the nooses on the desk in my school.

"Alter?" I asked tentatively, staring into my bowl of soup. "Would you ever consider coming out of retirement?"

Alter was seated and was wearing a new pair of glasses. He'd told me more than once how much he loved those glasses, so when he took them off and gripped them in one hand—something he often did when he was about to say something profound—I hoped he wouldn't squeeze them too hard.

He looked closely at me with his bright brown eyes, and the words came out with confidence.

"Well...I have some good news for you. Yesterday I received a call from a mother at your middle school. She wants me to speak there because she's so upset about this year's racist and antisemitic incidents."

I bolted upright, like I'd just received an electric shock. "Really? You're kidding me. Are you going to do it?"

"I am," he answered, smiling, "and I know you're happy to hear that. The nice woman said she's familiar with my speeches, and she wants me to do what I normally do as well as address the recent incidents at your school."

I was so delighted I jumped up from my chair and did a little dance, which made Alter laugh. Everyone who knows me knows that I love to dance—in the car, in the kitchen, when I get out of the shower... wherever. It's my way of showing how happy I am, and that afternoon, I was *so* happy. Alter's words and wisdom were like a breath of fresh air—and soon, my classmates were going to experience that, too.

On May 18, my mom, a few hundred of my peers, and I listened to Alter speak at Lakeridge Middle School. I'd seen his speaking routine so many times that I probably could have delivered it myself, but each time it was just the tiniest bit different. Alter would talk about his experiences, then gauge the audience's reactions. He'd see what moments they seemed to be leaning into and those they seemed to be struggling with, and he'd tailor what he had to say accordingly. Through it all, he wasn't afraid to push a little further with the difficult subjects, knowing it was important for people to hear the truth.

That afternoon, Alter weaved together his story with the events that had happened in our school, at Lake Oswego High School, and around the community, drawing parallels among them. He talked about the notions of accountability and consequences, and he wondered aloud whether the student who'd posted the "Easy-Bake Oven" sign had truly understood how much this hurt a person who'd suffered from antisemitism, like he had. In his entire speech, though, he never condemned anyone; he only denounced hate.

"I may have my pain," he said. "But I forgive those who caused it. I do not want revenge."

I thought back to a story from Alter's book. A few weeks after his liberation, Alter walked through the streets of Waldenburg, the town near the camp, and saw one of the concentration camp's former guards.

"Good morning, Mr. Schmidt," Alter said when he approached him. His voice was steady and level, with no hatred. The former Nazi immediately apologized to Alter, saying he'd been forced to become a guard and had only been following orders the whole time. In fact, he was disgusted by all that he'd done.

Alter didn't think twice about forgiving him.

I wondered: *If I'd been hurt as badly as he had, could I forgive, too?*

I looked around the audience. I noticed a sea of wide-open eyes and nodding heads. I usually saw this kind of reaction, but people seemed to be listening more intently. The room was quieter, and the air was more electric. With the energy in the room positively sky-high, I realized that Alter was making a bigger impact than he'd ever made before. His message felt urgent in a way it never had. He was showing people that their actions and words mattered *now*.

Alter usually spoke for about ninety minutes, then opened the floor to questions. Because of time constraints, there wasn't a Q&A planned, but I felt like half the crowd stayed afterward to speak with him. I noticed a few students even missed their bus so they could stay late.

My friend Hannah was one of them.

"Mr. Wiener," she said when I introduced them, "I've heard so much about you. Claire always calls you her best friend, and I guess I should be jealous of that, but I'm not."

Alter and I both started laughing. "Call me Alter," he said. "Any friend of Claire's is a friend of mine."

As I walked back to my locker, I saw a few students talking near the water fountain. I couldn't make out all the words and didn't want to seem like I was snooping, but I could hear phrases like "I shouldn't have said that" and "Apologize tomorrow." I could sense genuine remorse on my classmates' faces, like they were coming to grips with the consequences of whatever it was they'd said or done in the past.

Right in my own school, Alter had changed the hearts and minds of my fellow students, and they were ready to act on what he'd taught him. Suddenly, I realized I wasn't the only person who believed that the time to fight prejudice, racism, and intolerance was *now*. We were at a moment where we saw what was on the news and we didn't like it. We were ready to accept all kinds of people and work against all kinds of oppression. My friends, my fellow students, and I didn't want hate. We wanted to be like Alter: better, not bitter.

Chapter Nine

WE NEED A MOVEMENT

"I HOPE YOU HAVEN'T DECIDED THAT JUST BECAUSE you're now a teenager, you have no time for an old man like me," Alter joked to me just as the summer before my eighth-grade year started. I had turned thirteen on July 27, and my parents had taken me and my friend Amanda to Disneyland. I hadn't seen Alter for a few weeks.

"Of course not," I answered, laughing. "Never."

"So, did you have fun at Disneyland?" Alter asked. I'd sent him a postcard while I was gone, and I was delighted to see it sitting on the shelf below his Wall of Fame.

"Oh, yes!" I answered. "I always do."

———————•———————

My dad has a special talent for winning prizes (like concert tickets) during radio giveaways, and a few months back he had won an all-expenses-paid trip to Disney. My family *loves* Disney. Actually, that's an understatement. My parents had a subtle Disney wedding theme, I named the two cats I got for my third birthday Jasmine and Belle, and I dressed up as Disney characters almost every Halloween. So even though we live almost a thousand miles from Anaheim, California, we'd made Disneyland our family vacation as much as we could.

"I was thinking all vacation about your speech at Lakeridge in May, though. I mean, when I wasn't riding roller coasters."

Alter laughed. "Oh, really?"

"Yes," I answered. "That speech was a real turning point. The students were just…different. They paid more attention."

"Is that right?" he asked. "Was it because I wore my new tie?"

I laughed.

"It was a nice tie," I answered, "but that's not it. After the noose incident and the awful 'Easy-Bake Oven' poster mess…and everything else…I think people are realizing there's something wrong with the way we treat each other. The way we *feel* about each other. And that it's not just because of things happening in other places. It's here. It's everywhere. The world has changed, Alter. And we need to *do* something."

For a second, I worried I'd opened my mouth too soon. Alter was ninety, and he wasn't getting any younger. But he'd taught me to always be honest and never hide my feelings, so I knew speaking my mind was the right choice.

"I agree," he said after a pause. Then his brow furrowed up, like he was getting lost in a thought. "Let's keep thinking."

Whatever Alter and I came up with, I knew it had to empower students, letting them make up their *own* minds based on their *own* experiences. I wasn't sure what our plan was yet, but at least I was positive Alter and I were on the same page.

"So, we'll keep fighting, keep standing up for what's right? No matter what happens?" I asked.

"Of course. No matter what." He leaned forward to pat my hand, and I noticed how soft his touch felt, despite all his many years.

I tried to remember his reassuring words—and the gentle yet worn human contact he offered—when it felt like the world fell to pieces later that school year.

On February 14, 2018, a nineteen-year-old former student of Marjory Stoneman Douglas High School in Parkland, Florida, walked into one of the school buildings carrying a semiautomatic rifle and started shooting. Six minutes later, he'd left seventeen students and teachers dead and seventeen wounded.

This was far from the first school shooting I'd seen on the news. It wasn't even the first that *year*. But the student reaction was something I'd never witnessed before. The students who survived immediately created the hashtag #NeverAgain to protest gun violence, and they started a movement—at first online, and then quickly in person. They held a rally *three days* after the shooting. The next day, another group of students protested at the White House. Soon, teenagers demonstrated at the Florida Capitol building, urging companies to boycott the National Rifle Association (which dozens of them did), and, one month after the shooting, other young people led a national school walkout. More than one million students walked out of class to take a stand against gun violence—and I was one of them.

Ten days after that, between 1.2 million and 2 million people in 800 locations in the United States (including me and Aunt Sue) participated in the March for Our Lives protest in support of gun control, and the demonstrations were broadcast around the world. The Parkland survivor X González[1] stood on the stage in Washington, DC, for six minutes and twenty seconds—the length of the shooting—partly speaking and partly in total silence. Tears of sadness and rage streamed down their face much of the time.

I asked Alter the weekend after the march if he had watched X González's speech.

"I did," he answered. "That speech was one of the most impressive things I have ever witnessed."

I was always interested in Alter's opinions about people and events, and I was curious to hear his take on the protests. Parkland felt deeply urgent to me. These

---

[1]   Although they now go by X González, at the time the student went by the name Emma.

were people *my age* and it could have been me standing in the halls of Parkland as shots rang out around me.

"What was the most powerful part to you, Alter?" I asked.

"It is the fact that students are standing up all around the country—no matter how far away from Parkland they live! I am so impressed they are speaking out. Your generation is becoming different, Claire. I can feel it."

Alter shifted in his chair and took a sip of his smoothie. Then he placed it down on a side table, sat back, and crossed his arms. He had a look of determination on his face that I hadn't seen before, and his energy was positively electric.

"I have been speaking in Oregon and Washington since December 2000," he said. "I've also given virtual presentations around the country. I have met with church groups, synagogues, community groups, and prisons. I've even spoken to youth prisons. Now *that* is hard."

I nodded and leaned closer to him. "That sounds really difficult, Alter. I can't imagine being imprisoned that young." Then I realized something and blushed. "B-b-but...you can."

"Unfortunately, I can. What I am saying is that in every audience I have spoken to, I've seen people change. They have decided to stay in school rather than drop out. They have chosen to be kind to their neighbors and appreciate their differences instead of discriminating against them. Now all I see is hate around me."

Oh no, I began to worry. *I thought Alter was excited about something. Now he sounds so defeated.*

He must have seen the concerned look on my face because he spoke up.

"I told you I would never give up, Claire. This is my country. This is my home. After I left Poland, I moved to Israel hoping to build a new life, but I went there mostly because it was safe and secure. I am not sure my relocation was a conscious decision; I just went. When I left for the United States in 1960, I decided to live in New York City to be near other survivors. And even though moving to Oregon was more my wife's choice than mine, I have made a home here. I have met friends and built a community. I have a purpose and a vision because this is my *home*."

I scooted toward the edge of my seat. My strong, optimistic friend seemed like he was only getting started.

"I will *not* see the progress I have made go backward," Alter said defiantly. "I will *not* go back to a place where people hate their neighbors and turn against one another. So my question is: Is our response loud enough, Claire?"

I smiled and thought of X González. Like them and everyone at Parkland and around the country, I wanted change. I wanted it *now*.

"It's not, Alter."

"The world is telling us to be more public," he said. "Students are telling us to act in a bigger way. It's time. We need a movement. We need to make *laws*."

I agreed!

But what could we *do*? He was an old man, and I was just an eighth grader. Kids don't have a voice and can't make change, right?

Tell that to X González and the students at Parkland. Alter and I *did* have a voice, and we were going to use it.

PART TWO

THIS IS FOR
OUR FUTURE

Chapter Ten

✦

LIGHT A FIRE

Ever since I'd asked Aunt Sue why we didn't learn about the Holocaust in middle school, I couldn't shake the feeling that this was a *big* problem. Alter, more than anyone, agreed.

"Some people will argue that elementary or middle school is too young to teach about this part of history," he said not long after our conversation about the March for Our Lives. "But I firmly believe you're never too young to learn about kindness, tolerance, acceptance, embracing diversity, and anti-bullying. These are all the principles that can help prevent genocide."

Mom and I were at Alter's, and the three of us were talking about what, exactly, we could do.

I looked up and adjusted my glasses. "I know, Alter," I agreed. "But I feel a little powerless. We can't *force* schools to teach about the Holocaust."

He shook his head slowly. "It's not easy to make change in the government," he said. "I have pushed for legislation mandating Holocaust education before, and nothing happened."

"You mentioned this a few years ago, and I really want to hear more about it," Mom said—more impatiently than normal—from her seat on the couch. I looked toward her and noticed Alter's slippers on the floor next to her feet. They were parked neatly where they always were when Alter wasn't wearing them.

"Oh," Alter said with a sigh, "I guess I should finally tell you. A few years back I met a man who was planning to run for state senate, partially on the platform of mandating Holocaust and genocide education across the state. He lost the race, and the issue disappeared along with his campaign. I've spoken to so many other leaders about the need for education, too, and they always nod and agree and say they'll try to make it happen. But nothing ever comes to pass. Sometimes I follow up and never hear from them again."

I could hear the disappointment in his voice, and I hated that I felt that way, too.

Alter had always said that the potential for a genocide was right in front of us. History had proven that genocide takes root and springs from hate speech, and when people feel like it's their right to say terrible, intolerant things about other people—on the internet, in the halls at school, at home, or anywhere, really—they tend to find other people and groups who will join in with them.

"It's like a wildfire," Mom added. "Hate starts small, then it spreads until the whole forest is destroyed."

I didn't *want* a wildfire. I wanted the type of fire Alter's stepmom had spoken about when she'd said, "There are two ways to deal with the cold—put on a coat to be warm or light a fire so that others can be warm, too." That kind of fire brought people together. A spark from that fire would inspire and motivate individuals for *good*.

But how could I build that blaze?

A few years earlier, I'd taken part in one of Lake Oswego's favorite community charity events. At what was called Lakewood Bandstand, ten local "celebrities" learned a classic dance like the foxtrot or the cha-cha with the help of professional dancers. After weeks of practice, these locals and their professional partners performed in front of a live audience, and all the money from the ticket sales went to charity.

It was basically *Dancing with the Stars*, Lake Oswego style.

One year, one of the designated charities was the National MS Society. The event organizers needed someone who'd raised money for the organization to dance, and I couldn't believe it, but they chose me! All summer I practiced the Lindy Hop, a swing dance, with my partner, and on the night of the event, I dressed up in a fancy black dress, plastered my biggest smile on my face, and jumped, swung around, and even flipped (with the help of my partner)! I didn't win, but I had a *blast*.

I also got to meet a lot of interesting people from my community, including a member of the Lake Oswego School Board named Bob Barman. Over the years, Bob and I had sometimes run into each other at community or school events, and he was always kind.

So when Mom and I brainstormed ways we could get a politician or leader in the community to help us push for Holocaust and genocide education, the first person who sprung into my mind was Bob.

"Of course!" Mom said. "That's a great idea!"

"I think I still have his email address...."

Mom's face broke out into a smile. "I love it."

Bob would definitely know what I needed to do to move forward.

Even before I finished my homework or answered any emails that night, I found Bob's address in my contacts and wrote him a note saying I had an idea for our local schools and that I'd love to get his thoughts. I didn't go into too much detail, but I mentioned Alter, our friendship and its effects on me, and how all the recent racial and antisemitic incidents in our schools confirmed to us the importance of better education.

I pushed send and crossed my fingers.

The next morning, Bob wrote back, and he was as friendly and helpful as I knew he'd be. By the time school ended that day, we had set up a time to meet.

Light a fire, indeed, I thought.

Chapter Eleven

DOWN TO BUSINESS

It was a beautiful, sunny late-May day when Mom and I sat down at a table outside Starbucks with Bob Barman.

I had placed my notebook and Alter's book in a neat stack on the table when I spotted Bob walking toward us. He was tall, with white hair and warm brown eyes, just like I remembered him. Mom and I stood up, and we each gave him a hug.

Then we were ready to get down to business.

"Bob," I said, slowly and quietly at first, "I mentioned in my email to you that I've become friends with a ninety-two-year-old Holocaust survivor named Alter Wiener." I slid his book across the table. "He wrote his life story in this book, and I hope you can read it."

Bob nodded his head to show his thanks.

I took a deep breath and cleared my throat. "Alter has given almost a thousand speeches talking about what he went through in the Holocaust. Even though a lot of what he discusses is hard to hear, his message is always one of hope. He speaks about the importance of education and how it's the best way you can fight bullying and hate. He and I both believe that if students learn about the Holocaust and other genocides around the world, they will grow more compassionate and understand the consequences of their words and actions. By teaching them about the Holocaust, we can prevent something like it from happening again."

Bob leaned in, like he was about to settle into the conversation.

"Claire," he responded thoughtfully, "this subject means a lot to me. One of my best friends from college is the daughter of a Holocaust survivor. Learning about her dad's experiences changed who I am and how I treat other people. This topic is *so* important for students to learn in school."

He gets it, I thought. But I didn't want to get too excited just yet, so I mustered up all my courage and decided to press him for information.

"You are on the school board, so you're familiar with the curriculum...."

Bob nodded his head.

"Are students taught about the Holocaust in class?" I asked. "I certainly haven't learned much. I've also done some research, and I can't find any mandate that the Holocaust be taught in Oregon schools."

Bob shook his head no. "I, too, did some research after you emailed me, and I don't know about the state level, but in this district, there's nothing about the Holocaust in the curriculum. There are lessons and suggestions about what to put on a reading list—like Anne Frank's *The Diary of a Young Girl* and a few other young adult books about the Holocaust—but there's no clear guidance."

"That's what I thought," I answered. I'm sure Bob could hear the note of disappointment in my voice.

"I'm upset about it, too," he said firmly. "More than that, I'm angry about all that's happened this year and in years past in our schools. It's time for healing and better education. It's time for Lake Oswego to think about the future."

I paused. It was go time.

"Well, Bob," I said cheerfully. "I hope I can count on you to help us push for curriculum change in this district. It would mean everything to me and Alter. It would be the fulfillment of all the work Alter has done since 2000. In fact, it would be the most important thing he's done in his *life*."

Bob didn't even pause before he answered. "As a member of this school board, I will absolutely, one hundred percent support you. You can count on me for that. But I want to urge you to aim higher."

I couldn't figure out what he was talking about, so I was relieved when Mom spoke up right away.

"What do you mean?" she asked. "Other districts?"

Bob adjusted his glasses, like he really wanted to level with us. "Not quite. I think you may be able to work up to state level. I know it sounds like a big reach, but it's possible, if you could bring this subject up to the legislature in Salem. I know just the person you should speak to, too."

Salem? I thought, my heart starting to beat faster.

The Salem that's the capital of Oregon? Like, where all the state laws are made?

"Who should Claire speak to?" my mom asked excitedly, probably sensing the fact that I was completely at a loss for words.

"You need to talk to Rob Wagner," Bob answered. "He's from Lake Oswego and serves on the school board with me, but even more importantly, he was also just appointed to the legislature. When I get home, I'll connect you with him."

"Oh, gosh, that would be great," I said fast because I wasn't sure I could catch my breath. Then I smiled and thanked Bob. He'd been such a massive help.

"You're doing a good thing, Claire," Bob said warmly a few minutes later when we all stood up to leave. "I'm grateful for it. Thank you for the book, too. I can't wait to read it."

When Mom and I got home I Googled Senator Rob Wagner. *Of course*, I realized. His was the name I'd seen on a few yard signs and in the news. Rob Wagner had been appointed to fill a seat in the state senate in January and served on the state senate's interim education committee. He was now running in the general election in November, and if he won, he'd serve a four-year term.

While elections fascinated me, I knew next to nothing about our state government. So I dove even deeper on Google. What I discovered was pretty easy to understand. Like the legislative branch of the federal government of the United States, Oregon's legislature is split between a house of representatives and a senate. Rob Wagner represented the nineteenth district, which includes part of Portland, a few suburbs like Lake Oswego, and some rural areas. As Bob had said, Rob had served on the school board since May 2017. I imagined it must be a lot of work to serve on the school board *and* in the state senate, but I knew that sometimes, the busier you are, the more you can get done.

Let's hope Senator Wagner wants to take on even more work, I thought, *because I have some ideas.*

Date: June 7, 2018, 4:41 PM
From: Bob Barman
To: Alter Wiener
Cc: Claire Sarnowski, Senator Rob Wagner

Mr. Wiener: I will do whatever I can to support your effort. I believe your history must be remembered and not forgotten. Thanks for bringing this issue to the forefront. Bob Barman

Senator Wagner: I personally hope you can introduce legislation to make this a reality. Sincerely, Bob

For a minute, I stared at the screen, not believing what I was seeing. Sure, I knew my mom was in the process of setting up a meeting with Senator Rob Wagner's office, but this felt *much* different. I hadn't even started high school, and I was on an email chain with a state senator who was being urged to introduce legislation that could change what Oregon students learn in school! I was no longer a passive bystander, wringing my hands about intolerance and cruelty. I was more than a participant in a march, a fundraiser, or a dancer at a local charity event. I was someone who had the chance to make a *huge* difference by putting a new law on the books.

This was incredible!

A few days later, my mom and I got confirmation from Rob Wagner's office: We would be meeting him at a local cafe on July 26, 2018, the day before my fourteenth birthday.

It was on!

CHAPTER TWELVE

THE OPPORTUNITY
OF A LIFETIME

THERE'S A STORY MY DAD LOVES TO TELL ABOUT when I was a toddler, and even though it embarrasses me every time I hear it, I have to admit it's pretty accurate. Dad remembers that one night after we'd finished up dinner, he decided it was early enough that he could take me to the local playground.

"We can't stay long, though," Dad said, holding my chubby hand tight as we walked down the street. "It's going to get dark soon."

I loved the slide, and as soon as the playground was in sight, I let go of Dad's hand and ran as fast as I could toward it. Instead of climbing up the ladder, though, I grabbed the slide's side and decided to scale up. I was only two, and I had been walking for just a year. My little legs hadn't figured out that crawling *up* takes a lot more strength than walking straight, so I grabbed the sides and climbed, then slipped, sliding back to the bottom. Not wanting to give up, I pushed myself up again and repeated the same steps: grab, climb, move my hands up, and climb more. I fell again and started to slip, and my dad ran toward me, saying, "Claire, let me help you."

"No!" I yelled.

I grabbed harder onto the sides, pulled, and inched up. Every time my legs buckled, my knees hit the metal, but I hardly noticed. I was going to make it to the top of the slide if it was the last thing I did. Probably twenty minutes passed, and the light started to fade as the sun dipped below the horizon. When I finally reached the top, it was fully dark. I didn't care. I celebrated by planting my diapered bottom on the top and sliding right down.

"Now it's time to go home," my dad said with a laugh.

Focus and determination like that were going to carry me through this meeting with Rob Wagner.

Like most other middle school students, I'd studied

a little bit of civics, but my understanding of how a bill becomes a law was pretty much limited to what I'd Googled. I was also *totally* in the dark about the goings-on in my own state. So, I hit Google again to find out.

What I learned is that, in Oregon, any proposed legislation must be introduced by a senator or a representative. This is called *sponsoring*. If a senator sponsors the bill, it's taken first to the state senate, and if a representative sponsors the bill, it heads to the state house. The proposed legislation could be an idea dreamed up by the senator or representative because it's something important to his or her constituents, or the idea might come to them from concerned citizens with a big vision. Like me and Alter.

I was meeting with Rob Wagner, so I was about to be only one degree away from finding a state senator to sponsor a bill.

State senate, meet Alter Wiener and Claire Sarnowski.

"Now, I love Lake Oswego, but I'm sure you know it's kind of a bubble," I found myself saying to Rob Wagner less than five minutes after meeting him.

Senator Wagner looked at me and smiled. I'd prepared so much for this moment that my anxiety had faded away almost immediately after he'd warmly shaken my hand.

"Absolutely, Claire," he said. "I know this well. I grew up here."

I nodded, then continued the words I'd rehearsed in my head a hundred times. "You probably know that racist and antisemitic acts have happened before in Lake Oswego—many times, unfortunately."

"I do," the senator answered. "My children go to Lake Oswego Junior High. As a parent, an elected official, and a member of this community, I'm concerned about all the incidents that have happened lately."

"Yes, Senator Wagner," I said, taking a sip of my chai latte. "And—"

"Please," he interrupted, smiling. "Call me Rob. I have a feeling we'll be working together for a long time."

I hadn't realized how serious and formal I was being until Senator Wagner...er, Rob...pointed it out. I shook off my last bit of tension, smiled, and then glanced down at some notes in my notebook. I'd done a little research....

"So," I started, "I suppose you know that, in this country, there are giant gaps in education when it comes to learning about marginalized people and the history of hate."

He nodded his head.

"For example, about two-thirds of millennials don't know what Auschwitz is, and students graduating high school today versus those who graduated twenty years ago are twice as likely to be unable to identify the meaning of the Holocaust. With the number of survivors alive getting smaller every year, we're at risk of forgetting the Holocaust entirely. This will absolutely happen if we don't teach it in school."

Rob nodded again, then reached for his cup of coffee. I looked over at my mom and saw that she had a huge grin on her face. I think that's because she could tell how confident I'd suddenly become.

I slid a copy of Alter's book toward Rob, just like I'd done with Bob Barman earlier that year. "I believe you're familiar with Alter Wiener, my friend who survived the Holocaust," I said.

"I am," he replied. "My kids have heard him speak. He's an inspiration."

The first time I heard Alter speak was on May 30, 2014, at Crossler Middle School in Salem. Mom and I were so excited, especially because Alter signed his book for us!

Summer 2018. Alter and me on the route he walked every day.

On September 25, 2018, Alter was given the seat of honor in the governor's office before our testimony. Pictured left to right: Senator Rob Wagner, me, Representative Janeen Sollman, Alter, Governor Kate Brown, and Senator Chuck Riley.

Alter gave his last speech, at my high school, in December 2018. Pictured left to right: Interim Superintendent Dr. Michael Musick, Alter, Principal Desiree Fisher, me, and Bob Barman.

On July 15, 2019, Senate Bill 664 became a law! This is Governor Brown holding up the signed original.

After Alter died, Hillsboro dedicated a bench to his memory. I often come here to consider life, the world, and the beauty around me, just like Alter and I did when we were together.

"He has changed my life and is the reason I feel so passionate about this subject," I continued. Then I handed Rob a set of papers that explained the curriculum that other states had mandated.

"Right now," I said, "there are ten states in the United States that mandate Holocaust education. They've implemented it not only to honor the six million Jews who died during World War Two, but to ensure that history isn't repeated. As you know, education is the key to making a better future not just for students, but for the world they'll lead someday."

Rob looked down at Alter's book and began to page through it. Then he eyed the materials I'd given him and flipped from one sheet to another.

"Claire," he said kindly, "I am so impressed. I will start reading Alter's book as soon as I get home, and then I'll set up a meeting with him, as you and Bob suggested I do. I can't wait to talk to him."

Rob explained to me that he had many Jewish neighbors—people whose voices he needed to represent as a member of the legislature, but also simply people he cared about. "Their history is extremely important to me, and I listen to them. Their history is vital for us to learn and for our children to learn, and education is central to that. We are deeply lucky to have Alter in this area because there really isn't a survivor community. I take a personal interest in this, and it extends beyond my kids and my work in education. The Holocaust feels very real and very urgent to me."

"How is that?" my mom asked.

"I recently traveled to Israel as part of a nationwide delegation of state legislators, and I went to Yad Vashem, the World Holocaust Remembrance Center in Jerusalem. There is one gallery there shaped like a cone, with photographs of people lost in the Holocaust wrapping around the wall. I stared up at them and saw photographs of one person after another, extending toward the sky. The symbolism was so powerful it almost knocked me over. Then I walked outside and saw a railroad car on a road stretching down a cliff. It's a memorial to the millions of people who were deported from their homes."

"That sounds amazing," I said. "I would love to go there. I haven't even been to the Holocaust Museum in Washington, DC, and it's one of my biggest wishes."

"Claire," Rob said, lowering his gaze. "I have thought about that museum every single day since I was there. Visiting it was one of the most powerful experiences of my life, and I felt the pain of all those deaths and the weight of that horrible history. It caused me to reflect on how I can be an active advocate on educational issues, and now I understand how essential it is for students to learn about the Holocaust because it will change their lives. It certainly changed mine."

I took a deep breath. "So, what do you think our chances are of getting support for Holocaust education at the state level? Bob has already given his commitment to getting the Lake Oswego School Board behind the idea."

"You have my full support," Rob answered without missing a beat. "The next step is for me to talk to my colleagues and try to get a hearing scheduled. In the meantime, we'll need to develop a plan."

"So we'll keep talking?" my mom asked.

Rob extended his hand across the table and shook Mom's hand. Then he turned and shook mine.

"You have my word."

"Rob," I said, trying to sound calm and collected

instead of how I actually was: so excited I thought I might climb onto the table and start dancing. "Thank you. This is the opportunity of a lifetime. I know I have tons to do, but can you tell me what's next?"

"I can," answered Rob with a smile. "Get ready for your civics lesson."

Rob then gave me the short version of how a bill becomes law in Oregon. Here's a shorter version of the short version:

SOMEONE HAS AN IDEA
FOR A BILL!

THE BILL HAS A SPONSOR IN THE
LEGISLATURE.

TESTIMONY

LAWYERS AND EXPERTS WRITE THE
ACTUAL BILL.

THE BILL GOES TO A COMMITTEE AND
TO THE BUDGET OFFICE. IF THE COST

TO TAXPAYERS WILL BE TOO HIGH,
CHANCES ARE THE BILL WILL
STALL OUT.

THE COMMITTEE REVIEWS THE BILL AND
MAY HOLD PUBLIC HEARINGS. IF THESE
HEARINGS LEAD TO CHANGES IN THE
BILL, THE WORDING IS REDRAFTED OR
AMENDED.

LAWYERS AND THE BUDGET OFFICE
REVIEW THE BILL AGAIN.

A COMMITTEE VOTES ON IT.

IF IT DOESN'T PASS: GAME OVER.

IF IT PASSES: THE BILL GOES TO THE
HOUSE OR THE SENATE.

REPRESENTATIVES DEBATE IT.

A VOTE IS HELD.

IF IT DOESN'T PASS: GAME OVER.

IF IT PASSES: THE BILL THEN GOES TO THE OTHER SIDE OF THE CAPITOL, WHICH MEANS THAT IF THE BILL STARTED IN THE HOUSE, IT HEADS TO THE SENATE. IF IT STARTED IN THE SENATE, IT GOES TO THE HOUSE.

HEARINGS

TESTIMONY

DEBATE

VOTE.

IF IT DOESN'T PASS: YEP, GAME OVER.

IF IT PASSES: THE BILL GOES TO THE GOVERNOR'S DESK, AND THEY DECIDE WHETHER TO VETO IT OR SIGN IT. IF THEY SIGN IT...THE BILL BECOMES A LAW.

Whew! I thought after I finished listening to Rob. It was a lot to keep up with, but I knew Alter and I could handle it.

"Now, Claire," Rob said. "All of us—you, your family, Alter, my staff, and I—have a lot of work to do to get support for possible legislation. But if we get to the point that this legislation is likely, I think it might be helpful for you and Alter to testify at the committee level, in Salem. You made such a compelling case to me today about why this legislation is important, and I think you might make a big impact on the education committee."

I'd done public speaking in the past, for the National MS Society, and while it was sometimes scary, I actually really loved it. But embracing my civic duty and helping shape public policy was activism on a whole different level. Speaking in the state capitol to people who made the laws that affected everything from the roads we drove on to the classes taught in public school...that was...I couldn't even put it into words!

"Hang on, there's just one thing," Rob added. "You're going to need to pitch this bill to the *interim* education committee first. They hold one or two meetings before the session starts, to learn about upcoming bills. Their next meeting is at the end of September."

That was less than two months away!

It was time to get to work.

CHAPTER THIRTEEN

✦

GRATEFUL

LESS THAN TWO WEEKS LATER, MY MOM AND I arrived at Alter's and found him dressed just a little more nicely than usual.

"Oh, you're wearing your suspenders," I said with surprise. "And no slippers! We're not going to Salem *today*, you know."

Alter laughed. "It's not every day you get to meet a state senator, Claire. You have to look your best."

Rob Wagner had emailed Alter not long after our conversation to set up a meeting with him, and the day had finally arrived. Rob had agreed to come to Alter's apartment, which was a good thing because Alter was growing increasingly frail, moving just a little more slowly every time I saw him. He was still taking his daily walks, but if he wasn't feeling steady or if it was icy outside, he used his walker. Alter said he didn't want to take a chance and exert himself any more than he had to.

The three of us were still standing in the doorway when Rob pulled up and parked. He stepped out of his car with a big smile on his face, then said hello to me and my mom. As he walked toward Alter, his smile grew even wider.

"Mr. Wiener," he said, extending his hand, "it is such a pleasure to meet you. I read your book the day Claire gave it to me, and it affected me deeply. Thank you for sharing your important story."

"Thank you, that means so much to me," Alter answered, as polite and gracious as he always was. "But please call me Alter. And, please, come inside."

Naturally, as soon as he shut the door, the first question Alter asked Rob was: "Would you like a smoothie?"

"Yes, please, that would be wonderful," the senator answered. "I'll have whatever you're making."

As he sat down at the table, I could see Rob's eyes scanning Alter's Wall of Fame, with its diplomas, awards, and photos of Alter's loved ones. He seemed to pause on one of the newer items, one of Alter's most prized possessions: a copy of a statement with Alter's name on it, which US Senator Ron Wyden had presented to him in April, and the framed US flag that had flown above the Capitol in Alter's honor that day. My parents and I were in the audience at the ceremony. "He represents the best of Oregon values," Senator Wyden said while introducing Alter. In the statement itself, which is now forever in the Congressional Record, he had written, "There is a concept in Judaism called *tikkun olam*, which means to repair the world. Truly, I can think of no bigger way to describe Alter Wiener's work than repairing the world. Every time he shares his story, more people understand the horrors of Nazi persecution and the inhumanity of the Holocaust. People also understand the importance of tolerance, pluralism, and inclusion, and they see the power of the human spirit to endure."

Then Rob's eyes settled on one picture that was fading with the passage of time. It was a young boy wearing shorts and a button-down shirt, reclining in the grass.

"Is that you in that photo?" Rob asked when Alter

returned and handed him a smoothie. "I think I recognize it from your book."

"That's me," Alter replied. "It's the only photo I have of myself from my childhood. A neighbor gave it to me after the war."

"Don't you use other photos in your slideshow?" Rob asked.

"I do," he said, "but they were from my extended family and cousins. Every photo *I* owned was taken away when I went to my first forced labor camp." He paused. "A labor camp and a concentration camp are different, you know. At a concentration camp, you are meant to be killed. So they strip you naked, take everything you own, and hurry you off to the gas chambers as quickly as possible."

Rob looked solemnly at Alter. "You went to a labor camp, however?"

"Yes," Alter answered, "at first. There I helped build a gasoline plant for the Germans. I was forced to carry cut trees on my back all day, sometimes six or seven days in a row. If a prisoner fell down dead next to me, I had to carry him on my shoulders, too."

Alter turned his gaze to me. I closed my eyes and

looked down, soaking in the horror of what Alter had said. This was far from the first time I'd heard Alter describe a camp like this, but it still shook me to my core every time.

Rob asked Alter a few more questions after that, then they settled into that steady rhythm of conversation that Alter and I always had. They talked about current events, and then they spoke about their kids. Alter mentioned his career as a bookkeeper and an accountant in New York City, and then Rob said a few things about his career in education. The conversation turned to the legislation now and then, but it was never centered on that. Rob and Alter were just two human beings getting to know each other and learning about their different experiences in life.

"I want to show you something, Rob," Alter said at one point, after about an hour. He stood up unsteadily and made his way to his bedroom, which was just off the living room. He opened a drawer near the bed and reached inside, removing a three-ring binder that he brought to the table. I knew what was inside.

"These are some of the letters I've received from people who have heard me speak. Here," he said, pointing to one. "This young boy said he was planning to move away from his family because he had given up on them. He was already packing his things. Then he heard how I'd lost my father, and it caused him to realize how hard his father tried. He decided to stay with his family because of that."

I smiled, then reached over and pointed to a letter I'd seen before that I particularly liked.

"Oh, yes, thank you, Claire," said Alter. "This letter is from a young person who lost her mother. I lost my mother, stepmother, *and* father. She said hearing my speech helped her grieve. Do you mind if I read it?"

"I would love that," Rob answered.

Alter began to read in his thick accent.

My mother recently passed away from ovarian cancer... I thought the pain I endured was tremendous... but your talk today really showed me how fortunate I am to have my dad, my grandma, my family.

I'd seen this letter probably twenty times, but each time its effect was more powerful.

"I have saved about four hundred letters in total," Alter said. Then he smiled. "I won't read them all to you today. You'll be here for a week."

"I wouldn't mind that, Alter," Rob responded. "But I think you would."

We all laughed. I knew we'd meet again, and I knew it would be soon. Rob had told me earlier that he'd learn the date for the interim education committee meeting any day now. He expected it to be in late September—only a few weeks away—but the precise time had not been set.

"In the meantime," he told Alter, "think about what you might want to speak about. And start collecting email addresses for all your friends so they can come to the meeting and support you. The committee will need to see that this bill has massive support from the public."

"That should be no problem," Alter responded.

Rob paused. "I know it's a lot of work for someone who is as busy as you are. So, I'm grateful."

"Busy?" Alter sighed. "Always. In fact, I'm too busy to die." Then he smiled and opened his arms to give Rob a hug goodbye.

CHAPTER FOURTEEN

✦

YOU'VE GOT MAIL!

MY MOM'S BIRTHDAY IS AUGUST 20. THEY SAY THAT the older you get, the less you want to acknowledge the fact that another year has passed, and that's true for my mom. She *hates* celebrating her birthday. As the holiday lover in the family, though, I won't put up with that! Every year, Dad and I spend *months* thinking of just the right present for her, and on the night of her birthday, it's our family tradition to go out to dinner at a place she picks. This year, we were going to Stanford's, a neighborhood favorite. We'd be joined by my grandma and Aunt Sue.

In Oregon, most schools start in late August, so I wasn't doing much the day of her birthday except buying some school supplies and thinking about what I wanted to wear to the restaurant that night. It had been such a good summer, but I was ready to go back to school. I was starting my first year of high school at Lakeridge, and I felt like I was beginning a new chapter. It was a chapter that involved me putting more good out in the world. It was a chapter in which I could make a difference in my best friend's life and in the community I loved.

Maybe even the *state* I loved.

The only issue was that Alter and I hadn't heard from Rob yet, and I was getting anxious. I wondered: *Maybe he wasn't able to get a meeting scheduled?*

I pushed the worry out of my mind—at least temporarily—and told myself this was Mom's night. We had a *great* dinner. Mom rolled her eyes when the waiter brought out the cake and groaned when we started singing "Happy Birthday," but I knew how overjoyed she was to be with family. She couldn't stop talking about how delicious her dinner was on the ride home, and when we walked into our house well after dark, she turned to me and Dad and thanked us.

"I love you both so much," she said. "That was a wonderful birthday."

I had just changed into my pajamas when I decided to check my phone one last time before I went to sleep. Holding it in one hand as I perched on the side of my bed, I looked down, and there was an email from Rob Wagner. It was addressed to Alter, but I was cc'd.

"Mom! Mom!" I yelled, racing downstairs to the kitchen, where I knew she was cleaning up before bed. "Rob Wagner just emailed, and we have the date for the hearing!"

Mom put down a dirty dish and pulled me into a huge hug. She squeezed me hard, then stood back and looked at me.

"When?!"

"September twenty-fifth at two PM!" I practically screamed. "It's at the Oregon State Capitol. Rob says we'll have a total of fifteen minutes to present testimony. A few minutes for him, then five to seven minutes for me and Alter to talk!"

"Claire," she answered, clearing her throat. "That's in a month. I don't care if it's my birthday and I'm ready for bed. We have to email Alter *now*."

In the days after we found out the date of the hearing, I felt like I had pushed *fast-forward* on my life. Everything moved *so* quickly. I started taking notes about what Alter and I might want to say in our speeches, and I made lists of all the pertinent details we should tell the friends and family we'd be emailing about the hearing, as well as all the things we'd ask from them. I set up a Gmail address specifically for emailing people and receiving responses, and I started to write down all the names of people I wanted to invite.

Our requests were these:

1. Can you attend the hearing?
2. Can you send photos related to Alter or your experiences with the Holocaust?
3. Can you send documents or a letter describing your connection to Alter or the Holocaust?
4. If you have no connection to Alter or the Holocaust and simply believe in the importance of our legislation, can you write a letter saying as much?

5. Finally, can you spread the word about what we're doing? Awareness can be as vital to a cause as advocacy, and people need to know that our movement is out there.

I made clear that the committee needed to understand that this legislation wasn't just *our* pet cause. It was the express desires of hundreds and maybe thousands of people all across Oregon and even around the world.

My mom walked into my room one morning before school started, while I was busy typing up some notes and sending some emails.

"Claire," she said. "Do you remember Jackie Labrecque, the reporter Alter met a few months ago at the Café Europa event?"

"I do," I answered. "She loved Alter."

Café Europa was an event—held in various cities around the world—that brought Holocaust survivors together. It was named after a café in Stockholm that a survivor had founded after the war and that had turned into a gathering place for fellow survivors. Alter had participated regularly in Portland's Café Europa years earlier but had stopped going. This had been his first time back in a while, and he'd been interviewed there by a reporter from the local TV station KATU.

"Well, get ready," Mom said dramatically. "Jackie wants to interview Alter again about the legislation. She wants to interview you, too."

"Really?!" I asked, half in disbelief. A TV interview? Being on the news was a *huge* opportunity for us to build support for our cause. "When?"

"August twenty-fourth," Mom answered. "Which is tomorrow."

Oh my gosh! I thought. *I don't even have time to worry. I guess I've just gotta do this!*

I *shouldn't* have been worried because the interview went really well. Alter was a natural in front of the camera, with quick, catchy phrases that summed up his message perfectly.

"A wise person is someone who learns from their experiences," he told Jackie. "But the wisest person is someone who learns from somebody else's experiences."

Boom.

I'd actually done a few TV interviews before because of my MS fundraising. In fact, my mom has embarrassing videos of me at four or five, talking on the news about Walk MS, and I cringe when she shows them to people! That night in late August, though, I didn't want to take any attention away from Alter, so as I held his hand, I directed all the attention to him.

"He's living history," I said. "There's nothing like talking to him."

Alter was eloquent and persuasive, discussing our friendship and how we'd become interested in enacting legislation in the state. Together we got the point across of why passing a bill was so important to everyone's future—and how people across the state could help.

That weekend, I went over to Alter's, just like always. This time, we cut our catch-up conversation short and got right down to business.

"I think I should focus on gathering and organizing testimony, photos, and everything else everyone sends," I told Alter. "I can also answer everyone's email questions. You have all the connections, though. I think we'll have to use your contacts to reach out to everyone."

"If you want me to write to anyone, I would be happy

to do that," he answered. "I spend hours a day responding to emails. It is so important to always write back. My stepmother, Rachel, taught me that, and she was right."

"I know, Alter," I said with a smile. "You always say that."

My mind wandered back to all the times I had written to Alter. Never—not even once—had I gotten the last word. If I tried to end an email exchange with something conclusive, like "Bye! Talk to you later," he would still write back. If I said, "No need to write back!" he would still write, "Okay!" It was hilarious and one of the things I loved most about him.

Even on email, though, Alter was slowing down. He wasn't like me, who could dash off a response (with just my thumbs!) in fifteen seconds. Alter took five minutes to write every email, and they were careful and precise, showing how much he really cared about people. He now had to take breaks after sitting at the computer because it was too much for his eyes and too much for his fingers. I knew there was no way Alter could sit and draft emails for the seven hundred or so people he wanted to write to because he'd be tempted to personalize each one. He needed his rest.

"I have an idea," I said. "If I can get access to your email address book, I can export your contacts and send the emails about the hearing, the need for testimony, and more, all by myself. You won't have to do anything, Alter."

"That sounds like a good idea," he responded. "Let's work on this now."

Unfortunately, Alter was about as far from a computer expert as you could be—which made sense considering his age. I'm okay with technology, but I don't understand anything about AOL, so I knew this was going to be a challenge.

"I can find contacts on Gmail and pretty much every other email service, but I'll need to look at your computer to see if I can figure out AOL," I said.

Alter motioned me toward his computer desk. "Let me log on, and then you can sit here."

Alter entered his username and password after he offered me a seat next to him. When I scanned the AOL home page, though, I realized I couldn't find what I needed just by looking at the screen. I asked him if I could have the keyboard, and after he handed it to me, I Googled "how to export contacts from AOL."

Nothing that came up made sense.

"I think we're going to have to call AOL customer service," I told Alter. He nodded, and I pulled out my phone and dialed their customer service number.

AOL might be one of the internet's oldest email services, but they take security just as seriously as any other tech company. When the customer service representative answered and I explained the situation, he said that he had to speak to Alter first.

I put my phone on speaker, and the representative began talking.

"I'm going to ask you a security question, Mr. Wiener. My question is: What was your first car?"

Alter's brow wrinkled up, and he shot a look of confusion my way.

"Who sent this question?" he asked just a little too loudly. "I have never even driven a car!"

I put my hand over my mouth and started to laugh, and that made Alter laugh. Within five seconds, we were both doubled over, and my sides began to ache. I had heard Alter laugh a thousand times, but this was the first time we'd experienced true belly laughter.

"Sir," the representative said seriously. "Sir! Mr.

Wiener! If you can't answer that question, can you give me your credit card number?"

Alter's laughter caught in his throat, and he gasped. "I am not giving you my social security number over the phone!"

"He said credit card number, Alter."

"I'm not giving that, either!" he answered.

"But...," the AOL representative protested. "This is a secure line."

Alter was clear, and he didn't hesitate. "I am a ninety-two-year-old Holocaust survivor," he declared. "I simply do not give out my credit card information to strangers."

I heard a pause, and I figured the representative was consulting his employee manual about what to do next. Or he was calling his manager. What came out of his mouth next was the last thing I expected.

"That is so interesting," he said softly. "I've never spoken to a Holocaust survivor."

Alter perked up. "You should read my book! It's called *From a Name to a Number*, and you can order it online."

Alter and the AOL customer service representative continued their conversation for a good five minutes.

The rep asked Alter a few questions about being a survivor, then Alter asked him about his family. The rep talked about his children, then his mom, and Alter offered up a story about his stepmom and all the lessons she'd taught him. Then he pivoted to his speaking career, saying that it brought him more satisfaction than almost anything he'd done in his life.

"Speaking is how I met Claire," he added. "So, if you need her help getting you the information you requested, I give her my full permission."

I rolled my eyes, knowing that nothing is ever that simple when it comes to cybersecurity. Even though Alter had thoroughly and genuinely charmed AOL customer care, I still had to walk him through five more security questions about account numbers Alter had no memory of. It took another fifteen minutes, but we figured everything out. Before the representative ended the call, he made a point of saying one last thing.

"I enjoyed talking to you, Mr. Wiener," he said. "I learned so much and can't wait to read your book. Have a wonderful day. Thank you again for using AOL."

That's Alter, I thought to myself. *He can bond with almost anyone.*

CHAPTER FIFTEEN

✦

LIVING TESTIMONY

MAYBE IT WAS BECAUSE OF THE BELLY LAUGHS, OR it might have been the fact that Alter trusted me enough to let me break into his address book with all his security passwords and account numbers. Whatever happened that day, something changed between us. Alter and I had always been close in the four years we'd known each other, but now we were on a mission together. We weren't just talking about homework or current events or Alter's past; we were *doing* something. We had a cause, and it was an amazing cause.

I went home that afternoon fired up to get started. With Alter's address book safely emailed to my Gmail account, I printed out all his seven-hundred-plus contacts. As I pored over them, I couldn't believe what I was seeing. I called my mom over so she could look.

"Mom," I said, pointing to the printed contacts. "Alter made notes about each person in his contacts list. See? He noted their birthdays, wedding anniversaries, the day their first child was born...even work anniversaries."

Mom smiled. "I wonder why he does that."

"I'm sure he sends people emails on those days," I answered. "I mean, he never ever forgets my birthday. I wake up every year and there's an email from him."

"Me, too," Mom added.

The following Saturday, I brought a highlighter to his apartment so we could mark up the most important names.

"Alter, you are so organized," I remarked as I placed the contact list on his table. "I mean, I've always known that, but seeing these contacts really brings it to life."

"Claire," he answered, "I worked as a bookkeeper and an accountant. Those are jobs that require organization. In fact, I once told my boss that if I couldn't find something in twenty seconds, he should fire me immediately."

"I take it you were never fired?" I asked.

"I worked for him for twenty years, till he passed away. Now let's look at these names."

I smiled and pulled the cap off my highlighter.

"This is the daughter of a survivor who passed away last year," Alter said as we looked over the first page. "Ah, she was a wonderful woman. So is her daughter. I am sure she'll be able to write testimony or send photos."

I highlighted her name and email address.

"And this is the son of the second wife of a survivor I knew in Queens. We used to take the train into Manhattan together...."

At this rate, I was a little worried that going through seven hundred contacts was going to take days. But part of me didn't mind because hearing about Alter's friends was like discovering another side of his incredible life. He had teacher friends and student friends. He had a friend who was the dean of a local law school, and he had a neighbor who was a nun.

"She met Pope John Paul the Second," Alter said. "He grew up near me in Poland. I wish I had met him."

All of Alter's friends sounded fascinating. And he

assured me all of them had powerful voices and would lend their support to our bill.

After we narrowed down the list, I drafted emails, explaining my connection to Alter so the recipient wouldn't think my message was spam. Then I described what we were doing and how they could help.

I sent over four hundred emails that first week, and I remember thinking, *I have never been so busy.* The day I went to register for my high school classes—which also involved picking up my textbooks and getting my school picture taken—I was away from my desk for only about two hours. When I returned, I had forty emails responding to my blast. They said things like:

Here is my testimony and a few photos!

Please say hello to Alter!

We will be there for the testimony! When you know what time it will be, please tell me!

The emails that poured in were so moving, and I spent hours reading through what people wrote.

Everyone had something nice to say about Alter, and much of it brought me to tears. Alter had a huge effect on people, and his generosity and hope for a better future were contagious.

I shared everything that came in with Alter—like the testimony my new friend, Chanelle, wrote. I'd had a few classes with Chanelle but had never been very close to her—until now.

Dear Oregon State Senate Education Committee,

My name is Chanelle Buck, and I am a 14-year-old student at Lakeridge High School. I firmly support the teaching of the Holocaust and genocide for students in Oregon. I am sure many other students who have heard genocide survivors feel the same way that I did when I heard the survival story of Alter Wiener two years ago. I had limited knowledge of many of the horrors and crimes that occurred during genocides including

the Holocaust…33% of millennials still
don't believe these atrocities happened.
The Holocaust is not an event we forget;
we must work together to learn from
these horrible events and preserve the
memories of those who perished….

Alter was always so happy when he heard words
like this.

"Oh, that's wonderful," he would say. "I will write
Chanelle and say thank you."

When I got home that night, I forwarded everything to the Oregon Legislative Information System,
which is the legislature's central database for bills and
testimony. The senators on the education committee
could now log in and read the beautiful words that
Alter's friends had written. If they made half the impact
on the senators that they'd made on me, I was *sure* this
bill would pass.

Chapter Sixteen

BEAUTIFUL EMOTIONS

As a child growing up in the Soviet Union, I don't remember learning about the Holocaust or about any of the Soviet genocides. It was forbidden to do anything but praise the Soviet regime, it was forbidden to talk about the Soviet–Nazi alliance prior to 1941 and their joint invasion and occupation of Poland in September of 1939 that started WWII. The memory of the victims of the Soviet regime was kept alive primarily outside of the Soviet Union and inside the hearts of the survivors who could not share their memories freely while the Soviet Union existed. Only after the fall of the USSR and the opening of the Soviet archives by some post-Soviet states, it became possible for researchers and historians to talk to the survivors and study historical records. . . . I am grateful to the scholars and researchers and volunteers for preserving this history and I wish I had the opportunity to study it at school. I hope that students in Oregon will soon have such opportunities to learn about the Holocaust, to learn about Soviet and other genocides.

—Testimony from Tatiana Terdal, Oregon Representative, US Committee for Ukrainian Holodomor Famine- Genocide Awareness

I walked into Alter's apartment holding this testimony—plus a stack of about thirty more pieces of paper—in my hands.

"Alter!" I held out the testimony from Tatiana Terdal toward him. "Look at this. It's *fascinating.* I started reading about the history of genocide in Russia and the suppression of education during the Soviet years because of what she wrote. I had *no idea.*"

"Ah, yes," Alter replied. "This will help our cause."

He put the piece of paper down on his square table and gave me the strangest look. It was a mixture of curiosity and childlike excitement. I looked down and could see a folded piece of paper he was clutching in his right hand.

"Alter, what is that?" I asked.

"Please," he answered, "I need your help."

He pressed the piece of paper into my hands, and I opened it. It was an email I'd written him a few days before—but he'd printed it out in color.

"Umm, Alter. Why did you print this out? And why is it in color?"

"I want you to tell me how to get this," he said, pointing toward a few words in my email.

I scanned the email again and could not for the life of me figure out what he meant.

"What are you talking about, Alter?" I said sweetly, not wanting him to worry that I didn't understand his accent or was disrespecting him by thinking he was being strange (which he was). "Are you referring to something in my email?"

"This," he said a little more insistently as he pointed again. I squinted my eyes, and I realized he was directing my attention to the small red heart emoji I'd put in my email.

"That's an emoji, Alter," I said.

He grabbed my hand. "Let's go."

Alter led me to his computer and motioned for me to sit down in the rolling chair at his desk. I did as I was told.

"I want an emotion like you put in this email. Please," Alter insisted.

"Alter," I answered, trying not to laugh. "It's *emoji*, not *emotion*."

"Fine," he said, sounding a little bit irritated. "I still want it."

I held back another laugh. "Okay," I said. "Just remember last week when I tried to figure out your email account. This could be tough because I really don't understand AOL. Besides, emojis are meant for phones, not computers. You'd have to search for an emoji and then cut and paste or drag it from some-where else. It's a lot of work for an email."

Alter leaned forward and looked me in the eyes, then smiled. "You are my technical confidante, Claire.

If you can figure out AOL, you can figure out anything. I believe in you. You can do it."

I searched for a good five minutes and finally got what I needed. When I turned to Alter to tell him, his eyes lit up.

"You found it, Claire! I knew you would!" He gently nudged me. "Show me how to do it so I can practice."

After I showed him, he wrote an email about nothing in particular to my mom, and at the end of it, he signed it with a heart emoji. Then he added a wink emoji. Following that was a smiley face.

"So many beautiful emotions," Alter said. "I love this."

After we scanned all of the emails I'd received, it was time to talk logistics.

"I think we're in a great position," I said, "but we should start to consider next steps. First, Mom and I wanted to get some stickers made so we can pass them out before the hearing. People can wear them to show their support."

"That sounds wonderful," Alter answered. "Maybe you should put my book cover on them."

"That's a terrific idea," I said, my mind racing. "And we have to write our speeches. They are supposed to be seven minutes long each. You speak, then I do." I'd already been thinking about what to say, and there was *so* much. How was I going to sum up all of my thoughts and feelings about Alter and this bill in seven minutes?

"I'd love for you to read mine when I'm finished writing it," Alter said. "I'm going to start it next week."

I could feel tears forming in my eyes. "Of course," I answered. Then I paused again to catch my breath. "We're really doing this, Alter. We're going to Salem in a few weeks, and we're going to push for legislation mandating Holocaust education in Oregon. This isn't just a dream anymore—"

Alter interrupted me, then reached across the table to pat my hands. "I know, Claire. It isn't a dream. It's real."

CHAPTER SEVENTEEN

STRAIGHT FROM THE HEART

IT FELT LIKE I WAS THINKING ABOUT WHAT TO SAY to the interim education committee every second of every day. When I'd had to speak in public in the past—which I did to help kick off Walk MS a few times—I'd decided not to prepare anything formal. That might sound a little stressful (and, well, it kind of was), but I really wanted my words to come from my heart. Once I carried bulleted notes with me so I wouldn't forget to mention something or someone, but all the other times I simply opened my mouth and started talking.

I really wanted to do that for this hearing, but the committee requested my testimony beforehand, so I had to prepare *something*. The issue was: I needed it to be as authentic as if I'd made it up on the spot.

One night a few weeks after I started school, I sat down to organize my thoughts. I reflected on all that Alter and I had been through for the last four years, from me breaking my ankle to him struggling to mend his relationship with his sons. I remembered the first time I heard him speak, when I was struck by how strong he seemed, despite his small size. I thought about the ball cap he gave me, the taste of that matzo ball soup, and all the laughs I'd had after his silly jokes. Then I remembered what had happened recently, when Alter had tripped and fallen on a tree root that had broken through the sidewalk outside a local hotel.

"I had to get stitches, and I broke my glasses," he told me and Mom. "But I don't want to sue anyone."

When Mom and I came over and saw how badly he was hurt, with a black eye and a huge gash on his forehead, we tried to convince him that he needed to alert the hotel so that no one else would trip, either. Finally, Alter relented. On a sunny afternoon, he and I walked hand in hand to the front desk, and Alter told the staff and manager what happened.

"I've suffered through pain, but I don't want anyone else to suffer. Not your hotel, not anyone walking down the street, no one."

"We will fix the problem right away, Mr. Wiener," the manager said, almost in tears. "Your kindness and honesty are unparalleled. It's not every day someone meets a man like you."

That was Alter. Pretty much every memory of my time with him left me with the same warmth the hotel staff had felt.

I opened the voice memo feature on my phone, and started speaking about what Alter's friendship, Holocaust and genocide education, and the notions of kindness, peace, and being better, not bitter, meant to me. Then I cut my words down to a few minutes, transcribed them, and sent everything to Alter and the committee.

My speech was straight from the heart.

Alter wrote to me after he received what I'd written.

Dear Claire,

This is an excellent testimony. You are talented, sensitive, knowledgeable, brilliant, compassionate, very pretty, and much more.

I am deeply moved by your complimentary comments about me in your testimony. You are precious.

With everlasting love
Alter Wiener

When Alter sent me what *he'd* written, I could tell he'd been a little more methodical and deliberate than I'd been.

"I am so used to giving the same presentation over and over," he told me. "It's hard for an old man like me to come up with something new to say."

Of course his speech was well thought out and highly organized (no surprise about the organization!). I couldn't *wait* for the day we would testify.

I've always loved working hard. When I raised money for MS, I made a point to increase my goal every year.

After I raised $900 my first year, I upped my goal to $1,500. Then $9,000. When Dad and I played tennis at the courts down the street from my house, I always tried to do something new or achieve a personal best: Maybe it was for my ball to clear the net ten times in a row, or maybe it was for me and Dad to rally for three minutes straight.

Preparing for our interim education committee appearance was different, though. There was more organization, more multitasking, more leadership, more...everything! People expected me to have the answers to every question, I'd get frustrated if I didn't write someone back fast enough, and this was on top of all the homework I had. I was *exhausted.* Instead of pushing snooze three times like I wanted to do, I jumped out of bed an hour early and logged onto my computer so I could answer any testimony-related emails that had come in overnight. I began to long for a Saturday when I could sleep past 6:30 AM.

Luckily, my friends, family, and school couldn't have been more supportive of me. And I felt like my classmates really *got* what it means to try to make a difference. We'd witnessed what teenagers like X

González, Jamie Margolin,[2] and Malala Yousafzai[3] had done to make change happen. Starting in August, we'd seen Greta Thunberg on the news, standing outside the Swedish parliament holding a sign that demanded action on climate change (and Greta said *she'd* been inspired by the activists at Marjory Stoneman Douglas!). We were all realizing that civics wasn't just something you learned in school. The law was a living thing that even *teenagers* could influence.

Suddenly, it was cool to be politically active.

Kids at school had seen my interview on KATU or had read about me and Alter in the newspaper, and they came up to me in the halls to ask me about Alter and what we were doing. Even upperclassmen who would normally turn up their noses at the idea of talking to a freshman approached me. People told me so many stories, from the visit they had made to the United States Holocaust Memorial Museum in DC

---

[2]   The founder of Zero Hour, a youth organization that fights against climate change

[3]   A Pakistani human rights activist who was shot in the head by a Taliban gunman when she was fifteen. When she was seventeen, she was awarded the Nobel Peace Prize for her work, making her the youngest laureate (meaning winner) ever.

to the survivor they'd met at their grandma's nursing home. They teared up when they recalled the racist slur they'd endured the year before or the antisemitic words they'd seen online. There were also people like Chanelle, who I'd gotten really close to because of her interest in what Alter and I were doing. She offered to skip school so she could watch me and Alter testify. Today, Chanelle is one of my best friends, and her mom, Marcelle, might as well be a second mom to me.

People in middle and high school are so quick to form cliques, and often those groups center around good looks, popularity, or how much money you were raised with. But in the weeks before Alter and I testified, kids my age came into a whole new light for me. I realized we could come together through mutual passions and shared causes. What exists on the surface is—by its very nature—shallow. But the values and ideals that lie deep in our hearts are what can bond us for the long term.

Straight from the heart, indeed.

CHAPTER EIGHTEEN

✦

EMPOWERED TO ACT

"IF THIS BILL BECOMES A LAW," ROB WAGNER SAID to me during one of our many exchanges before the committee meeting, "it will probably be implemented in middle and high schools."

That made sense to me.

I did a ton of research as I dreamed about what the curriculum might look like in Oregon. One thing I was sure about was that this law should enforce what I learned was called a *full mandate*. A full mandate states that something passed into law *must* happen. It's not a suggestion, in other words. Rob Wagner felt the same, and we were hoping the legislature would agree.

But we didn't have to outline a specific curriculum

to get this bill passed. Instead, it would be "in development," with certain goals laid out in writing. School districts throughout Oregon weren't all the same, and their curricula shouldn't be either.

"Each district might take a different approach about what they teach," Rob explained. "Some might spend more or less time on a subject depending on their students' backgrounds and needs."

I thought for a minute about what that might mean. "So, a district with a large Southeast Asian population might focus a little more heavily on Myanmar, for example?[4] There's ethnic cleansing happening there right now, so it's really important to teach students about it, especially if they're from that part of the world."

"Absolutely," Rob agreed.

We both felt it was crucial to make clear that the

---

[4] Myanmar, also known as Burma, is a large country in Southeast Asia, bordering Bangladesh, China, and Thailand. Its people elected to end military rule in favor of democracy in 2010, but that didn't stop the ongoing civil war that's been going on in the country since the 1960s. In fact, that war has been called the world's longest civil war. Myanmar is the site of many human rights violations and frequent ethnic cleansing, especially toward the Muslim Rohingya people in the northwest part of the country.

legislation shouldn't *only* include resources to teach about the Holocaust, since there have been many genocides throughout history.

"History does tend to repeat itself," Rob said. "Students need to know what leads to genocide, like racism and hate speech. By learning about the *issue* of genocide—and the many wide-ranging massacres throughout history—they can begin to understand that one event never truly stands alone." Then he paused. "One thing we have to be careful about, though, is making it clear that a district shouldn't compare acts of genocide. The Holocaust killed six million innocent Jews, but what happened in Turkey[5] and Bosnia[6] and Rwanda[7] and elsewhere is equally horrific. Atrocities are atrocities no matter what."

I looked down. "It's sad," I said with a sigh. "The

---

[5]   In 1915 and 1916, between 664,000 and 1.2 million ethnic Armenians were massacred in the Ottoman Empire, now Turkey, in what's been called "the first genocide of the twentieth century."

[6]   Between 1992 and 1995, about 100,000 Bosnian Serbs were killed in the largest ethnic cleansing in Europe since the Holocaust.

[7]   From April to July 1994 (only 100 days!), leaders of the central African nation of Rwanda's Hutu people led a campaign that killed more than 800,000 Tutsis. Hundreds of thousands of Tutsi women were also raped in the massacres.

Holocaust may be the best-known genocide in history, but the issue of human extermination didn't start and end with it."

It was true. Even though after the Holocaust people around the world had begged and pleaded that we should never forget and never let something like that happen again, it had. Again and again and again. That's why young people needed to grow up holding the knowledge and the tools to root out hate.

Education will provide those tools, I thought.

We knew there are so many different ways to approach this, but ultimately the lessons would need to be compelling enough to spark meaningful discussions in class. Students should think and connect, relating the issues of the past with the issues of today. And while the lessons might feature tragic, upsetting stories like Alter's, we wanted them to relate tales of triumph as well.

"If students learn about the strength and resilience of the human spirit after war or genocide, they'll feel empowered to act," I told Alter. "Everyone wants to know that beauty can grow from darkness. They want to feel hopeful about the future."

"That's pretty much the lesson of my life," Alter answered.

While I'd been studying up on Holocaust and genocide education around the United States, I'd also learned so much about what other states have and have not done. For example, California was the first state to pass a law mandating state-wide Holocaust education, and that happened in 1985. Their law also required them to teach about the Armenian Genocide. The state of Texas passed legislation much later, in 2018, and their law mandated a Holocaust Remembrance Week, when the history and the lessons learned from the Holocaust would be taught. Michigan's law extended as far as the state tests, saying that questions about the Holocaust and the Armenian Genocide had to be included.

My heart swelled when I thought of all the possibilities of what this curriculum could do and how it might work in each district. I was only fourteen—the age at which Alter had dropped out of school—and I was being given the chance to influence what education might look like for students like me.

Alter was even happier.

"I think this bill is a second chance for me," he told

me the day we walked hand in hand to the nearby hotel (where he'd tripped), being careful to avoid uneven pavement. "Education has always been a ticket to freedom and a better life, but I lost that chance in the war. In America, I received my GED and took some college classes. But as I said to my employer once, the schools I attended as a young man were Blechhammer, Brande, Gross Masselwitz, Klettendorf, and Waldenburg...."

"Your five camps."

"Yes," he sighed. "But now I have a second chance to bring education to others. Nothing makes me happier than for a young person never to face the same obstacles I did. With education, they have *everything*."

Alter was right. Passing this bill wouldn't make up for all the years he should have been in school but lived in a camp instead, but it would put education firmly at the center of his long life.

This bill *was* for Alter—as well as for other survivors—to ensure that their legacy and past were never forgotten nor ignored. Equally, it was for all the current and future students in our state of Oregon. With education, they could have hope. With education, they could act and make meaningful change.

CHAPTER NINETEEN

✦

TOGETHER AS ONE

OH, WOW, I THOUGHT TO MYSELF AS I LOOKED UP the steps leading to the Oregon State Capitol. *I can't believe today's the day.*

I'd spent many school breaks at Aunt Sue's house in Salem, but I had never stepped foot inside the building that houses all of Oregon's government—*especially* not for something as momentous as making a speech in front of the legislature. I'd walked around the Capitol grounds, winding my way through the blue spruce, Douglas firs, Japanese maples, magnolias, and famous cherry blossoms that line its three massive city blocks. I'd stared up the steps leading to the giant white marble building, with its circular rotunda pointing up to the sky. And I'd looked in wonder at the bronze and gold-leaf statue of a rugged, bearded outdoorsman that's perched at the top. I'd noticed how he's holding a tarp and an axe, staring west. I had always liked that statue, which I'd always known as "The Gold Man." I didn't know till recently he had a real name—the Oregon Pioneer. But I hadn't thought much about his symbolism till the day of my testimony, when I realized something.

That statue is all about Oregon's past. We're here today because of its future.

And now it was time to shake off my nerves and convince some state senators to back our cause.

Unfortunately, during most of the morning of Tuesday, September 25, I had been totally on edge. At 6:00 AM, I shot out of bed, worried I'd overslept.

Of course, I hadn't. There was no way I could have. Even though it had been next to impossible to fall asleep the night before, I was way too excited to sleep in. This was *the* big day for me and Alter, and I was almost positive we were going to kill it.

The weather around Portland can be unpredictable

in the beginning of fall. Some days, it's rainy and cold. Other days, there's not a cloud in the sky, and the temperature is that perfect, crisp sixty-something degrees that makes you think of apples and Halloween and changing leaves. Today was *not* one of those days. By the afternoon, it was going to be sweltering.

Alter and I had planned what we were going to wear in advance. I'd settled on a sensible black sleeveless dress that I could pair with a sweater for the air-conditioned car ride and take off when we were outside. I'd never seen Alter wear anything but a suit, suspenders, and a tie when he spoke, so I wasn't expecting him to look dramatically different.

"I shouldn't wear my bathrobe?" he joked the weekend before. "Because that's what I'm most comfortable in."

I shook my head, thinking, *Alter, you get dressed up in a collared shirt even when you're not planning to leave the house.*

"Hi, Claire!" my mom said with a big smile on her face when I came downstairs. She was already dressed in a fuchsia-colored shirt that was so bright it made me happy. "Are you ready?"

"I've never been more ready for anything!" I answered a little too fast. The truth was part of me was terrified. What if the legislature laughed at me? What if no one showed up? Mom must have sensed my hesitation because she held her arms out, and after I walked to her, she enveloped me in a huge hug.

Mom and I had already packed everything in our car so we wouldn't forget a thing. We had a box full of stickers, each with a photo of Alter's book and the words I SUPPORT HOLOCAUST AND GENOCIDE EDUCATION on them. We had copies of Alter's books, my speech, a sign-in book for everyone who attended and wanted to receive periodic updates from me, and printouts of all the testimony and photos people had sent just in case anyone wanted to see them.

Now we just needed Alter.

Mom and I wanted to make it as easy as possible for Alter to get from our parking place into and around the Capitol, so when we picked him up, we brought his walker and decided to get a wheelchair when we got to the Capitol building. Alter did not object. After I helped him into the front seat, Mom put his walker in the back, and she returned holding three stickers.

"One for you, Alter. One for Claire. And one for me."
Each of us peeled the back off our stickers and stuck them on our chests.

The ride from Hillsboro to Salem took a little longer than an hour on the interstate, and as I nervously scanned the time on my phone to make sure we weren't running late, Alter peppered me with questions.

"Who's submitted testimony?"

"Did I tell you my old neighbor from Queens emailed me her support?"

"Are you as excited as I am?"

I was, but I was also busy going through emails! People were *still* writing me to tell me they'd be there.

A lot of people think of Oregon as totally mountainous, with the remains of Mount St. Helens or a snowcapped Mount Hood looming in the distance, but the stretch of land between Portland and Salem isn't really like that. Both cities lie in the Willamette Valley, with the Willamette River cutting south as rolling plains span out from its banks. As we drove, the overpasses, hotels, and chain restaurants that dot most interstates around big cities like Portland began to recede, and the clusters of evergreens that grew on the sides of the highway became thicker. At one point, we passed a large stretch of farmland populated by cows and horses, and I glanced up from answering emails and gazed happily out the window at them. Then, just as the exits became fewer and farther between and I started to wonder if we were about to head into the middle of nowhere, the suburbs of Salem began.

Then we reached the Capitol. *This was it.*

There were so many people on the Capitol steps, and they weren't just tourists. Other groups had arrived in Salem to support bills that were passing through a committee, just like we had. I looked around and saw a collection of men, many of them with beards, baseball caps, and blue jeans. They wore matching T-shirts featuring an axe and a slogan.

"That's a loggers' union," my mom said as we began to head up the ramp with Alter in the wheelchair we'd picked up when we arrived. "I wonder what bill they're supporting."

"I'm not sure," I answered, "but I'd love to give them some stickers."

I walked over to the loggers, introduced myself, and handed them a few stickers. Each man thanked me and placed a sticker on his shirt, right next to his union pin.

"Good luck today!" one of them said, waving. Alter, Mom, and I waved back.

Even though the interim committee meeting was due to start at 2:00 PM, we'd arrived at 10:30 AM and we had a full schedule ahead of us. We planned to meet Rob in his office, do an interview with a reporter from the local station, KATU, and then head to the senate room thirty minutes early so we could greet the people who'd come to support us. I wheeled Alter up the ramp, and as I glanced around, I recognized the familiar faces of a few senators I'd seen online while I was doing research. I saw a few capitol police officers walking by, and I noticed the grassy grounds spreading out in front of the building, with people buzzing around from one place to another. My nerves started to settle as I realized how electrifying the whole scene was.

This is where laws get made, I thought. *And I'm going to be a part of it.*

Mom opened the door for me and Alter and followed

us slowly as I wheeled him toward the rotunda. Then I turned back to her, confused.

"Isn't there a metal detector we have to go through?" I was no stranger to the fact that politicians are frequently threatened by angry constituents—some of whom have guns.

"There's no metal detector here," my mom answered. "It's kind of amazing. Anyone can just walk in, go upstairs, and visit a senator or representative."

I looked up. The interior of the Capitol rotunda rises into a dramatic dome, and at the center are thirty-three stars that symbolize Oregon's entry into the United States as the thirty-third state. It was breathtaking, and I froze up, realizing the magnitude of what Alter and I were about to do.

I paused and turned so that I was facing Alter. Then I reached down and placed my hands on top of his.

"No matter what happens today," I said with a huge smile on my face, "we are together, as one."

"Always," my best friend answered. "Today and always."

When we found Rob's office, he was standing just behind his desk, waiting to greet us.

"Alter! Claire! Carol!" he said happily. "Come in."

Rob thanked me and Alter for giving him our speeches early, and he congratulated us on how polished and persuasive they were. Then he announced that he had a surprise for us.

"I know you have an interview with KATU after this," he said. "We'll show you where to do that. Afterward, though, the governor said she'd like to meet you in her office."

I looked over to Alter, and his eyes lit up.

"Kate Brown wants to meet with us?" he asked.

"Yes," Rob answered, smiling. "She said she'd be honored."

Our interview with KATU went by in a flash. The reporter couldn't have been friendlier, and she talked to Alter, then me. When she wrapped up the filming and wished us luck, one of Rob's aides ushered us out of the room, then led us to Governor Brown's office. I wheeled Alter across the green carpet into a giant, wood-paneled room. The governor stood in front of a massive wooden desk, with Alter's representative,

Janeen Sollman, and senator, Chuck Riley, standing there, too. Alter lifted himself up slowly out of his chair and walked toward them.

"I'm Alter Wiener," he said, smiling from ear to ear as he extended his hand toward Governor Brown. "I am honored to meet you."

"I have heard so much about you, Alter," she replied as she shook his hand. Then she looked at me. "You, too, Claire. It is a pleasure to meet you both."

I'd seen Alter happy before, but this was a whole new level of joy. He was beaming as the governor asked him about his speaking, our proposed bill, and his hopes and dreams for the future of education in our state. I knew how busy Governor Brown had to be, so I didn't take a second of it for granted. From the delighted look on his face, I could tell Alter didn't, either.

"I know you have to go to the committee meeting," she said after a few minutes, "and I have a meeting, too." She paused. "I look forward to signing this bill into law if the legislature passes it. Best of luck."

I thought Alter was going to faint right there on the green carpet. And maybe I was going to, too.

CHAPTER TWENTY

✦

ALL OF US

AS ROB LED US TO THE SENATE HEARING ROOM, I was petrified that nobody had shown up or that our speeches wouldn't be well received.

Please, please let the people who said they'd support us be here, I thought, as I opened the door.

I peered inside, and I couldn't believe what I saw.

The room was *full*. People spread from wall to wall and seat to seat, and men and women in business suits stood with their backs to the sides of the room. There was my family friend Tricia and my neighbor Ann from down the street. I saw elderly people sitting in folding chairs with their arms linked, and I spotted one of my favorite teachers, Mrs. Mauritz, who I'd had in kindergarten, first grade, and second grade. There were six-year-olds holding signs, their moms propping them up on their laps, and camera crews and newspaper reporters dotting the crowd.

People skipped work and school to come, I realized. *They* really *care about this cause, and they wouldn't be here if it weren't for me and Alter.*

Alter had gotten out of his wheelchair, and he walked down the aisle through the left side of the carpeted room. He greeted every single person he passed, hugging and thanking them for coming. I've never had a wedding (obviously!), but I can imagine that if I ever have one, I'll feel the way I did that day: overwhelmed but overjoyed. The crowd was an ocean of faces I knew and loved and seeing them made me so proud of all our work.

In the front was a long, semicircular podium, with a line of padded, high-back chairs facing the audience. *That must be where the senators on the committee sit*, I figured, even though it looked more like the courtrooms I'd seen on TV shows like *Judge Judy*.

Alter and I finally reached the rectangular table

where we'd be sitting, facing the senators. Much to my surprise, Rob was already there.

"There are *a lot* of people here!" Rob said. "I'm not sure I've ever seen this room so full."

I wasn't sure whether to be thrilled or intimidated, but I decided to go with thrilled.

"Will the senators be coming in soon?" I asked.

"Any minute now," he answered.

I sat down, with Alter to my left and Rob next to him. Seven senators walked in and took their seats, and the meeting was called to order. The chairman of the committee, Senator Arnie Roblan, explained the reason the interim education committee had come together: to hear issues that would inform them before the official legislative session began in January. No senator would introduce a bill that day, but they would in January, and what they each heard today would help them decide their vote.

Then he introduced Senator Wagner.

"I'll keep my comments very brief today because, as you can see from the audience, I don't think people are here to listen to me." Rob then pointed to me and

Alter, describing how he'd met us and why we were in the room that day. He said that as a Lake Oswego resident and school board member, he believed genocide and Holocaust education were vitally important to his community because racial and cultural intolerance had hit so close to home, so recently. He described the swastikas in the bathroom at Lake Oswego High School, and then he revealed, in all its terrible detail, the "Easy-Bake Oven" incident.

"We are losing our history," he added.

He described how less than 2 percent of 16 million World War II veterans are alive today and that the number of Holocaust survivors is dwindling, too. I looked over toward Alter—his wrinkled hands resting on the table and his eyes that had seen so much inhumanity looking forward—and I felt my heart sink.

I know I won't have him much longer, I thought.

Before Rob turned the microphone over to Alter, he talked a little about his trust of teachers and how he didn't want to write the curriculum. He pointed to other states and how school boards there were successful in partnering with community organizations and teachers to provide age-appropriate education that made sense to their particular schools. That was all Alter and I wanted, too. We had no desire to mandate *how* things were taught; we wanted only to ensure the education that would allow each community to grow a little stronger and more tolerant.

"Good afternoon," Alter began right after Rob finished talking. Then, without even pausing, he dove into his testimony.

For the next eighteen minutes, Alter's accent was thick—like it always was—but his voice was stronger than it had ever been. Almost immediately I saw one senator lean forward, as if he was so interested, he couldn't stand to miss a word. Alter began to recount the dreams he'd had when he was incarcerated. The first was that he wanted to be reunited with his family. Unfortunately, that never happened. The second dream was that he wanted to eat as much bread as he could.

"However," he went on, "I had never dreamt that one day I would be invited by legislators of a state in the United States who would be willing to listen to me in the presence of a distinguished audience."

Alter's politeness warmed up the senators, but I

knew how genuine it was. He was thankful in a million different ways to be in that room with them. So was I. Alter then talked about his early days in the United States, when he cleaned toilets for money during the day and went to school at night. He talked about becoming an accountant, then retiring and moving to Oregon. He discussed the beginning of his unexpected career as a speaker, starting in 2000, and the letters he received from people of all ages who'd seen him speak.

His life after the Holocaust had been joyous and full of promise, he said, and he'd passed that hope to others. Unfortunately, though, his horrible teenage years would never leave him.

"For me, the memories from the Holocaust are still fresh," he said. "The ashes are still smoldering. I'm tormented by memories even as I try to carry on with my life. I'm crying in silence. I'm still in pain. I'm tortured by nightmares."

Yet, he added, he refused to let that grief immobilize him, knowing deep in his heart that he simply *had* to keep going.

Suddenly, I realized something. That resilience was one of the things I most appreciated about Alter. He refused to think that anything was hopeless, despite what he'd endured. In his eyes, everyone held promise, and everyone could improve—especially through a good education.

I looked around the room and toward the senators, and I could sense Alter's positive influence washing over them. Their eyes were wide and full of wonder. Their breathing was quiet, and no one was looking at their phone or at the clock on the wall. Everyone in the room was feeling his impact, just like I had five years before.

I was so overcome with emotion over Alter's speech that when he finished up, I wondered if I'd be able to get my words out. I felt like my life had gathered and expanded into this one moment, and it was so packed with pressure and emotion that I might just pop. As Rob motioned toward me, indicating that it was my turn to talk, I could feel my voice begin to shake. Then I got the words out.

"As my dear friend Mr. Alter Wiener once said, 'There are two ways to deal with the cold. Put on a coat to be warm. Or light a fire so that others can be warm, too.'"

I kept speaking, trying so hard to be strong, but my voice started to crack. Tears filled my eyes, and when they began to stream down my face, I stopped talking. Then I apologized because I wasn't sure I could keep going.

"It's okay," Senator Roblan said, "take your time."

I saw Rob slide a box of tissues over toward me, and I took one, then dabbed my eyes.

You can get through this, Claire, I thought. *You can.*

I took a deep breath. Objectively, I knew there was no reason for me to be so emotional, but this moment was *everything* to me. Testifying here for something I cared passionately about was a once-in-a-lifetime opportunity.

I regained my composure and began to talk about the first time I'd met Alter. Just like it was yesterday, I remembered the feelings that had come over me when I heard his words, and I recounted what I'd thought then.

"How could such a wonderful man exhibit so much kindness after going through the horrors he'd endured?"

Then I recalled moments from our friendship. I mentioned that I'd heard him speak at least fifteen times, and each time I walked away with a new lesson about something. I learned gratitude, love, appreciation, compassion, and, most importantly, how to live life to the absolute fullest.

When I wrapped up my speech, I felt like my heart was going to explode. No speech had ever been so hard for me, but at the same time, none had ever felt better.

The room was quiet, and then Senator Roblan related that he'd gotten to know a Holocaust survivor who'd been used as a human experiment while she was in the camps. Just knowing her and understanding what she'd gone through had changed the senator's perspective about what was difficult in life, and it had turned him into a more compassionate person.

Then another committee member, Senator Sara Gelser, piped up and told us about when she was a middle schooler and a Holocaust survivor had come to speak at her school.

"I can still picture where I was sitting in the classroom," she recalled. "Those lessons shaped the way I think about people."

I had no idea I was walking into a room with so many like-minded people, I thought.

It was true. I knew the members of the committee would be kind, but they were *beyond* kind. They were genuinely invested in the mission and purpose Alter and I had walked into the room to try to relate.

When our portion of the committee meeting adjourned, we exited the room and greeted all the people who'd spilled out of it into the hall. I thanked everyone I could, and I gave more hugs than I could count. After about ten minutes, we all walked toward the rotunda, and when I found Alter, we gathered the supporters who were still there and took a group photo on the rotunda steps. We didn't walk out the door of the Capitol until at least 4:00 PM, and when Mom, Alter, and I finally situated ourselves in Mom's car, I felt what seemed like twenty knots of tension melt from my shoulders.

"Are you doing okay?" Alter said to me, leaning his head toward the back seat as Mom pulled out of the parking lot. "I thought you were wonderful, Claire."

I looked down. "Oh, Alter," I said with a sigh. "I don't know about that. I'm really embarrassed I cried."

"Now, *Claire*," my mom said with a hint of tough love in her voice that I didn't hear very often. "There is absolutely no reason to be upset because you did the best you could. You would have been deceiving everyone if you'd tried to cover up how you really feel."

I know she was trying to make me feel better, but for a second, I felt worse.

"Mom, you know I've never cried during a speech. I just…" Mom and Alter were quiet, allowing me to finish. "I poured my heart and soul into this day, and I got emotional all of a sudden. I wish I'd been stronger."

I heard Alter clear his throat, and I could tell he was preparing to say something important.

"When you show your emotions, Claire, you are not weak. Your tears demonstrated your passion. You were honest and inspiring to everyone in that room because you showed them how much this issue affects you. You should never ever be ashamed of your big feelings. They reveal the excitement and enthusiasm you have in your heart."

I wiped away my tears and smiled in relief. "Do you really think that, Alter?" I asked.

"I know that," he answered. "I spent my teenage years suppressing my emotions because I was a prisoner. Believe me, holding in so much made me feel weak. Now that I am an old man and can express my pain and my passion, I feel happy."

I took a deep breath and closed my eyes, partly from exhaustion and partly from relief. We'd done it. Now, all we had to do was wait for the bill to go to the full senate education committee.

CHAPTER TWENTY-ONE

✦

KEEP FIGHTING

"CLAIRE, YOU *HAVE* TO WATCH THE NEWS!" MY DAD insisted.

It was after 6:00 PM, and I'd just finished up the long ride back from Salem after the most intense day of my life. I was so tired all I wanted to do was run upstairs and take a long, hot bath. But Dad had already turned on the KATU nightly news and was perched on the couch waiting for me and Mom.

"I don't think they've aired it yet, so you're right on time."

A few minutes later, the face of the reporter who'd interviewed us came on the screen, and Mom grabbed my hand.

"There you are!" she shrieked. "You and Alter sound great!"

As I settled into the couch, I started to unwind. We *did* sound good, and everything about the piece was wonderful. KATU featured some of our testimony and picked the best clips from our interview. They were supportive and enthusiastic, and if I'd ever worried that the community wasn't on our side, I had no reason to feel that way anymore.

Maybe I didn't need that long, relaxing bath anymore.

When I arrived at school the next morning, my classmates were over-the-top happy for me.

"Claire!" I heard someone yell down the hall. "I saw you on KATU!" When I peered down the hall to see who was shouting, it was a girl I didn't even recognize. I can't tell you how many hugs and words of congratulations I got from everyone all day long. Teachers pulled me aside, students stopped me after class, and emails and texts poured in on my phone.

By far the biggest gift I got that week, though, was from Alter himself.

For years, I had talked about how much I wanted to visit the United States Holocaust Memorial Museum in Washington, DC. DC is a long flight from Portland, though, and with me being in school most of the year and busy with activities and tennis and friends during the summer, my family and I had never figured out a good time.

"I want you to go, Claire," Alter said on more than one occasion. "It is an extremely special place to me, and it's my greatest and final wish that you can travel there someday."

"I will," I answered. "I don't want you to worry about that. I'll get there at some point."

A few days after the interim committee hearing, I returned home from school and decided to check the mail while Mom parked the car. Inside were a few pieces of junk mail and a letter addressed to me. The handwriting was crooked and shaky, but it was unmistakable.

Why is Alter sending me a letter?

I couldn't wait, so right there in the driveway, I carefully slid my finger under the crease of the envelope and ripped it open. There was a check inside, made out to me, with the words "For your trip to the Holocaust Museum" in the memo line.

I knew I'd be giving that check back to Alter when I saw him that weekend, and I knew he'd laugh at me for it. He *never* understood why it was so hard for me to accept his gifts.

"Remember that a gift saved my life, Claire," he always said. "A brave German woman who worked in a factory with me, while I was a prisoner, secretly passed me a sandwich every day. Without that food, I know I would not have lived."

No matter what he said, I wasn't going to take his check, but I *would* make it to the Holocaust Museum one day. I promised him that. I just hoped my visit would be in time to tell Alter all about it.

During the first few months after Alter and I testified to the interim education committee, there wasn't much work for us to do. We waited to hear from Rob about when the bill would be introduced, and I spent my time reading emails from people who asked what was going on and how they could help. I always answered them, telling them that as soon as I had a firm date for the bill's introduction, I'd email them back with instructions about how to contact their senator to urge him or her to support it.

The fall was a waiting game, but that was just the way it was.

To be honest, I'm not sure I really minded. It wasn't that I'd accepted that the legal process is slow; it was more that I realized I had space and time to sit back and appreciate what I was grateful about in life.

On the top of that list was Alter.

Alter and I had been close since the first day we met. After the interim committee meeting, though, our friendship hit its peak. Maybe we felt like we'd been through something massive together—and we had. Or maybe it was because I broke down at the committee meeting, which showed Alter how vulnerable I was. Looking back, though, I think the reason was bigger than that. As Alter's body became weaker and older, he started to depend on me for strength. As I grew up, he began to realize he was passing his legacy on to me. Our bond felt deeper and more profound, and day by day, Alter could see that our efforts were *working*. His dream was finally coming true, and it was so much sweeter now that he could enjoy it with someone. Alter had hundreds and maybe thousands of friends, and I would never dream of saying that I was closer to him than anyone else. But something had changed, and he seemed happy—truly happy—in a way he hadn't before. We were two peas in a pod, content to talk about life, current events, or nothing in particular as we waited patiently for news of our bill. We were *settled*, and I think that's why the shock of what happened at the end of October affected Alter so badly.

On the morning of Saturday, October 27, 2018, my dad and I watched the news together, horrified.

At 9:50 AM, Eastern time, a forty-six-year-old man walked into the L'Simcha Congregation in Pittsburgh, Pennsylvania. Also called the Tree of Life, the synagogue was in one of the most heavily concentrated Jewish neighborhoods in the United States. The man was carrying four loaded guns, and over the course of one hour and eighteen minutes, he used them to kill eleven of the congregants who had come to worship during Sabbath services. The oldest of the victims was ninety-seven. During the rampage, the killer shouted, "All Jews must die!"

Alter and I had plans to see each other the next day, and when my mom and I arrived at Alter's parking lot, I had a bad feeling. He took longer than normal to come to the door. When he finally appeared in the doorway, the look on his face was grim.

"I'm glad you're a few minutes late," he said. "I've been reading the paper, and I think I needed a little more time to finish it this morning."

I looked inside and saw that Alter had spread out the Sunday *New York Times* on his table. The paper was open to a long article about the shooting.

"Yesterday was a horrible day," I said sadly. "One of the worst."

I walked inside, took off my jacket, and sat down, trying to make myself at home. I noticed that Alter hadn't put out any snacks on the table, nor had he offered to make us smoothies. He wasn't himself, and that became even clearer when he started speaking.

"It was the worst attack ever on a group of Jews

in the United States," he said. "Eleven people were murdered. And the killer's hatred of Jews was fueled by conspiracy theories and rumors he read on the internet. On the internet!" Alter pounded his fist on the table.

I wanted to cheer him up, so I tried my best to sound optimistic.

"Alter...this is why we're doing what we're doing. People need to know that all the hate they see online is destructive, and that half the ideas on those horrible websites on the internet aren't true. We want people to understand which news is fake and which is real, and we are telling them that history is real. The Holocaust is real because *you experienced it*."

My words didn't help. If anything, Alter started looking even more unhappy. He stacked and then restacked the newspapers on the table, then he took a deep breath.

"When I was liberated," he said slowly, "I thought the persecution of my people and *all* people for their sexuality, ethnicity, race, religion, and more would be over. I thought we had seen the worst during the Holocaust, and that there was no way we would ever go back to that. I was wrong."

"But, Alter—" I interrupted.

"No, Claire. Things got worse. An American shot Martin Luther King Jr. because he fought for racial equality. In Columbine, Parkland, Sandy Hook, and dozens of other schools, Americans shot *children*. Now someone is killing elderly Jews. Human beings commit thousands and thousands of crimes against each other daily, yet we don't see this news reported on the front page. How many people in the United States know about what's happening in Yemen?"[8]

I shrugged. "No one talks about Yemen in my school," I said. "I have a feeling most of my classmates know nothing about the humanitarian crisis there."

Alter closed his eyes and sighed. "In the past ten years I've seen more violence against innocent human beings than I did in the ten years before them...and then the ten years before that. I've spoken to so many people and groups, and I'm starting to think that nothing I've done has helped."

───────────────

[8] Yemen, an Arab country in Western Asia, has been fighting a civil war since 2011. Over 55,000 fighters and civilians have been killed in the war, and it's resulted in famine and disease that have killed over 17 million people. Some journalists, scholars, and politicians have called the crisis a genocide.

I reached across the table and placed my hand on top of his. "You *have* made a difference, Alter," I reassured him. "Look at all the letters you've received. Look at all those lives you've changed."

He said nothing. He just looked down and shook his head.

Alter and I sat quietly for a moment, and I began to wonder if any of my words had sunk in. Then I wondered if reassurance even mattered in the grand scheme of things. Alter was ninety-two, and his body was weak. He walked extremely slowly, he had trouble eating, and answering emails exhausted him. He'd battled grave illnesses, starvation, and the death of his entire family. Now he was supposed to fight a rising tide of intolerance within the country that had provided him refuge, a home, and a purpose? I just wanted my friend to be happy, but maybe I was asking too much.

"Claire," Alter said finally, the spark in his eyes returning just the tiniest bit. "I feel sick when I realize that shootings and acts of hate are normal these days. But I see you, and I see the hope you have for a better future. I witness your generation wanting so much to help. You're marching in the streets, calling senators, and fighting against climate change. When I was fourteen, I made a vow that I wouldn't let the Nazis kill me, and that I'd fight the rest of my life for a better world. I will *not* stand by and watch that hope die in you the way it died in me when I was young."

I sat up in my chair. "So you'll keep fighting?" I asked.

"As long as we're together," Alter answered, "I will."

CHAPTER TWENTY-TWO

✦

FOR YOU, THE WORLD

ALTER ALWAYS JOKED THAT HE WAS TOO BUSY TO die, but all kidding aside, he *was* too busy—and too tired—to continue his speaking engagements. In the fall of 2018, Alter hadn't spoken anywhere for about two years, except that day at the Capitol. But between the Tree of Life shooting and the positive momentum building around our Holocaust education bill, I had a feeling he might pick it up again.

"You've gotten so much great press about the bill," I told him one afternoon. "People keep telling me how interested they are in what you have to say. And after Tree of Life, I believe you *have* to say something."

Alter scrunched up his face a little and looked

around the room. "I've been thinking hard about this," he said firmly. "I have a duty to speak. So, yes, I will do it."

I knew it, I thought. In fact, I was so sure he'd take me up on my idea that I'd done some work in advance. "Why don't you speak at my high school?" I asked. "Don't be mad, but I've already talked to my principal, and she'd love to have you."

Alter agreed on the spot, and within a week, the Lakeridge High School administration set a date. He would be speaking in front of the student body on December 5. My elementary school, middle school, and now high school...Alter had visited all of them!

All my hard work that fall had built onto itself. When I emailed people to keep them updated about the progress of the bill, sometimes they came up with ideas to help spread the word more. For example, a close friend of Alter's who worked at the Hillsboro Public Library encouraged the members of all the library's book groups to write testimony. In late November, my junior high school put on a play called *And Then They Came for Me*, which is an adaptation of Anne Frank's story told through the eyes of one of her friends. The director asked me to talk to the actors and stage crew about the Holocaust and my friendship with Alter. The more work I did, the more work I generated, and it was an *amazing* feeling. Ever since I was a nine-year-old, winding my way through a middle school cafeteria with kids who towered over me, my life had changed in ways I never would have imagined.

Alter's life had changed for the better, too, but I knew his body had a hard time keeping up. I was cautious with him all the time now. Even though there was a spring in his step that I'd been worried was gone forever, I didn't want him to wear himself out. In the days before his speech at Lakeridge, I urged him to take more time to prepare than he usually did. He always brought a few boxes of his book to his speeches, signed on page three, right above his number: 64735. I knew he needed to start far in advance to get them all done.

"You're going to have to sign sixty copies, Alter," I warned him. "You are so meticulous, and I don't want you to underestimate how exhausting this might be for you."

Alter nodded his head and gazed into the box of

books. "It's a lot," he said, smiling, "but I don't want you to worry. I can do it."

On the Sunday three days before his speech, my mom checked her email on her phone just after we finished eating breakfast. I glanced toward her and saw a look of horror cross her face. Then she burst out laughing.

"Claire, come look at this," she said, holding her phone out toward me.

On the screen I saw an email from Alter.

Date: December 2, 2018, 5:34 AM
From: Alter Wiener
To: Carol Sarnowski

Hi Carol, I've been up all night signing books. My hands are cramping, but I've signed everything. —Meticulous Alter

I started to giggle, and Mom laughed again. Soon, we were both laughing so hard our sides hurt.

I was there to meet Alter when he and my mom arrived at Lakeridge High School on Wednesday, and I'd already arranged his books in neat piles and set up his slide presentation. As students filed into the auditorium and found their seats, I looked around the crowd and noticed that there were some younger children in addition to all the high schoolers.

They bused in kids from the elementary school, I realized. *There are students out there who are the same age I was when I first heard Alter speak.*

I sat back and smiled at the memory.

Our principal approached the microphone, and the room grew quiet. She briefly thanked Alter, then turned the floor to me. Now, it was my turn. I was planning to introduce Alter for the first time ever, and it was such an honor.

I wasn't even nervous.

After I said a few words about my friend, I talked about our bill and our recent testimony in Salem. I mentioned how important it was for students to care about world events and learn about even the darkest times in history. The Holocaust isn't just something in the past; the terrible events of years before affect everything about the present day, and Alter's impact on the world was living proof of that.

When Alter stood up carefully, I positioned myself near him so that I could manage his slide presentation. For the next sixty minutes, he spoke. His speech was shorter than usual, and I could tell he was a little rusty given that he hadn't delivered it in so long. But I was the only person who noticed. To the rest of the audience, Alter's message was just as powerful and moving as it had always been.

"Alter, that was wonderful," I gushed as he walked away from the podium and toward the steps.

"I'm so glad you came out of retirement for Lakeridge," my principal added.

Alter extended his arms and gave my principal a huge hug. Then he turned to me.

"For you, the world," he said, and he pulled me into his arms and gave me a kiss on the cheek.

CHAPTER TWENTY-THREE

✦

A MILLION TEARS

"I WISH I COULD RIDE IN THE CAR BACK WITH YOU," I answered, and I hoped Alter could hear the sadness in my voice. "I have a biology test, though, and I can't miss it. Mom is going to drive you."

"That's okay," Alter answered. "I'll see you next weekend."

Mom helped Alter out of the auditorium, and I walked toward my test. That evening after school, I caught a ride home with a friend. When I walked in the door to my house, I was surprised Mom wasn't there. I started my homework, and I heard her car come up the driveway an hour later.

"Where were you?" I asked my mom when she walked in. "I thought you'd be home hours ago."

"Alter made me stay to eat a bowl of matzo ball soup with him," she answered as she put her purse on the counter. "We kept talking and talking, and I finally said to him, 'Alter, I have to leave and go home to cook dinner. My family is expecting me.' "

"Yeah, I was starting to get worried," I answered, then smiled. "And hungry!"

Mom laughed. "Well, Alter was thinking about you the whole time. When I told him I had to leave, he walked to his refrigerator and pulled this out."

Mom opened a paper bag and removed a small Tupperware container. It was filled with matzo ball soup, and on the side of the container was a note. The handwriting was unmistakable: "For Claire."

"Alter apologized that he didn't put many matzo balls in my soup," Mom said. "But he knew how much you like them, so he gave you a few extra."

The following Tuesday, December 11, I really could've used some of Alter's matzo ball soup. I had three tests the next day, and I was so stressed out that tears kept filling my eyes. Mom was making dinner around 6:00 PM like she always did, stirring pasta or taking a roasted chicken out of the oven while KATU nightly news hummed along in the background.

"Are you okay, Claire?" she called to me.

"No," I said, and my voice broke. "I'm so stressed out. I have *hours* of studying to do tonight."

"Honey, you need to relax," Mom said reassuringly. "I'm sure you're overstudying. By the way, dinner's going to..." Her voice trailed off as I stood up from the couch and walked toward the TV. Something had just caught my attention, and I had to listen more closely.

"Oh, my gosh," I gasped. "A pedestrian was hit by a car and killed in Alter's neighborhood about an hour ago. I hope it's not one of his friends." I motioned her to come closer.

"It can't be Alter," she said as she walked quickly toward the TV. But I could hear a worried tone in her voice.

"There's no way, Mom," I answered, and I meant it. Alter always walked in the morning, and he spent his nights tucked away in his apartment with friends or on his computer.

Mom turned away from the TV, walked back to the kitchen, and opened the oven door. She took something out and slammed it shut. "I'm going to email Alter just in case," she said. "He always emails back in the middle of the night when he wakes up from his nightmares."

Poor Alter, I thought. For most people, sleep is a refuge, but for him, it was constant torment.

I slept fitfully that night, too. I crammed so hard for my tests that I didn't get into bed until midnight, then I tossed and turned and woke up for good right before five, feeling just as anxious and edgy as I had the night before.

When I left my room to go to the bathroom, I noticed the light next to Mom's bed was on, so I figured she must be awake, too. Sure enough, she got out of bed and greeted me in the hall. She looked like she hadn't slept much, either.

"I know it's probably nothing, but I never heard back from Alter last night," she said as she pulled the sash of her robe tightly around her.

I thought hard for a few seconds, and then decided

I had no reason to be worried. There had to be a rational explanation.

"Alter has a new caregiver who comes to help him on Wednesdays," I answered. "And today is Wednesday. She helps him with his emails, so he probably didn't answer anything last night because he knew she'd be there the next day."

Mom nodded her head. "That has to be it."

But I could tell she was already really worried.

Marketing was my first class of the day, and as I sat in my seat, my stomach was still in knots over the three tests I had to take that day. I couldn't concentrate on anything the teacher said, and twenty-five minutes in, I was relieved when someone walked into class to deliver the teacher a note.

I can close my eyes for a second, I thought.

The sound of a hand landing on my desk jolted me back into consciousness, and as I opened my eyes, I could see a typed note on yellow paper sitting in front of me. "Report to the office immediately," it said.

That's weird, I thought. *This never happens.* Then I noticed a word under "office." In small lettering, it read "bereavement."

I have been a good English student for as long as I can remember, but the meaning of that word didn't register with me. As I gathered my bag and headed out into the hall, I convinced myself I must be in trouble. Then I wondered if I'd left something important at home and Mom had come to drop it off for me.

I can count on one hand the number of times I've been called to the principal's office since I was in elementary school, so as I opened the heavy glass doors, my heart began to race. I felt like it was about to leap out of my chest as I walked in, and my hands started to sweat. I approached the secretary's desk and said my name, and a look of sadness crossed her face.

"I'm so sorry, honey," she said sweetly.

What was going on?

She motioned me back toward the principal's office, and when I opened the door and walked inside, the principal was standing behind her desk, with Mom and Dad facing her. They turned toward me. Mom was crying, and I looked over to Dad and noticed that he was crying, too.

"What is going on? Why are you here?" I was getting frantic.

Then I stared a little closer at my mom's face, and, suddenly, I *knew*.

It's Alter, I thought. *It's Alter.*

I burst out in tears and ran into Mom's arms, and as she hugged me tight, I started shaking. I don't know how long I stood there, but I was still trembling when she and Dad led me out of the office and helped me into the car.

On the drive home, Mom told me that Alter had been walking his usual route at 4:57 PM the night before, just about an hour before she and I had heard the news story about the pedestrian who had been hit by a car. It had been pouring rain and was almost pitch-black, and Alter was wearing a dark jacket and a hat. He wasn't in the crosswalk; he'd stepped just a few feet away from it because it was easier for him to get from the curb to the street that way. The driver who struck Alter hadn't seen him before the impact, and when the police came, no fault was found. The driver wasn't drunk, careless, reckless, or on his phone; it was just a horrible, devastating accident.

A million thoughts raced through my mind that day and every day after that. *Why had Alter been out so late? He always walked in the morning. Was he buying something? It couldn't be, I told myself. He wasn't carrying anything, and his refrigerator at home was full.*

None of it made any sense. Alter had *always* been so cautious crossing the street, and he was only five minutes away from his apartment. How and why could this have happened?

Unfortunately, there are some truths you'll never discover. None of us ever learned why Alter left his apartment that night, and I doubt any of us ever will. I cried a million tears that night and for months after, and many nights, I still do. But what I *do* know, deep in my heart, is that when Alter died, the fire he'd helped light inside me didn't go out along with him. In fact, it started to burn even brighter.

CHAPTER TWENTY-FOUR

✦

REMEMBERED

I DIDN'T GO BACK TO SCHOOL THE NEXT DAY. NOR did I go back the day after, or the day after that. I know I worked on details surrounding the bill, cried my eyes out, and corresponded with Alter's friends and family about his upcoming funeral, but I don't remember much else of what I did. I do recall Chanelle and Marcelle coming by to check on me, though; they were selfless and understanding when my grief was at its worst. And I can summon up memories of the kind classmates who texted and emailed me. They'd seen the news about Alter's death on KATU or in the papers, and the impact of his speech was fresh in their minds.

I know I made up my tests later, but I don't recall

taking them. I just know how tired I felt, and how exhausting it was to be pulled in the direction of school, studying, and keeping people informed about the bill, then back toward my devastating grief. My pain was worse than anything I'd felt in my life.

Alter's son asked me to give a eulogy at his funeral, and I chose not to prepare anything. I'd never spoken to Alter using a script, so I wanted to honor him by speaking directly from my heart.

Like a lot of elderly people, Alter had picked out his gravestone and his grave site years before he died, and it was closer to my house than his apartment had been. He and I had even joked about it that fall, not imagining how soon his death would be.

"When I die," Alter said, "you can visit me twice a week rather than once because I'll be so much closer to you."

I laughed then, and while it took me a few months, I started to laugh about it again. It's just like Alter to make me laugh through my tears, and to turn even the saddest things happy. He *is* closer to me now, and I visit him every chance I get. In fact, when I got my driver's license on October 8, 2020, the first place I drove was

Alter's grave. It just happened to be his birthday, and I wouldn't have missed that for the world.

After Alter died, the thing he feared the most didn't come to pass. Alter had always been terrified that education and awareness about the Holocaust would die with him. The exact opposite happened. On the day of Alter's funeral, dozens of people walked up to me in the synagogue. Some were people I recognized, like the nun who lived in Alter's apartment complex and the librarian from the branch near Alter, whose name was Cynthia.

"I told Alter every time he walked into the branch that I lived right near him and would be happy to scoop up his books for him," she said. "But he would not have it. 'No, Cynthia,' he always told me. 'I want to get out and see my friends, like you.'"

Others were people I'd never met before or whose names I didn't recognize. Almost all of them offered to help me in my efforts to get our Holocaust education bill passed in the senate. They wanted to write testimony, appear in person, carry signs, distribute stickers, and more. I'd worked hard to get media attention before Alter died, and reporters began to call me twice as much, saying they really hoped I'd keep going. Suddenly, I felt like Alter's spirit was stronger than it had ever been, and he was pushing me to make the dream he'd inspired in me come true. The words he'd spoken to me as we left the legislature rang in my ears, and I knew that, for him and for all the future generations of Oregon's students, I had to keep going.

"This is not for me," Alter had said, "And this is not for you. This is for our future. And this is for people like you, who are interested."

It turns out that the Oregon senate was even more interested, because on March 12, 2019, our bill passed unanimously. At the final hearing a few months before the official vote, the house education committee chamber was packed with Holocaust survivors, survivors of other genocides, friends, classmates, and people from the community whose faces I didn't recognize. My mom and aunt were there, too, supporting me like they always did. There was also a handful of white supremacists, Holocaust deniers, and people opposed to education mandates there in protest.

"Don't let them get to you," one of the representatives said. "They show up to the legislature anytime an education bill is up for review."

The collective strength in that room nearly knocked me over, and the whole time I wondered how Alter would have felt. I imagined he'd be filled with the kind of happiness he hadn't known since he was a child, before the Nazis stormed into his town. I thought of his smile as he walked off the stage for his final speech at Lakeridge, and I knew his joy in the senate chamber would eclipse even that.

I didn't think March 12 could be even *more* amazing, but I was wrong. That same day, Senator Wagner and Representative Sollman introduced a concurrent resolution in their chambers (the senate and the house, respectively) to recognize Alter and his contributions to the State of Oregon. It was a beautiful testament to his work and legacy and couldn't have come at a more perfect moment: just as his dream of getting a bill passed was well on its way. I'm pretty sure this massive recognition also gave the bill momentum, as it demonstrated that first-person educators like survivors are passing away, so someone has to pass the torch to the next generation.

The best way to pass that torch was through education, and our bill made that a reality. On July 15, 2019, Governor Kate Brown signed Senate Bill 664 into law while Rob Wagner and I looked on. On an easel next to her sat a framed picture of Alter, so he was watching over the signing, too. My best friend's dream had come true, and millions of children around the state he loved would never be denied an education about one of history's greatest tragedies, as well as about so many other mass atrocities in the world. Through the lessons Alter believed in so strongly, they would learn to make the world a better place.

Just like he did.

AFTERWORD

———◆———

On December 11, 2019—exactly one year after Alter died—a bench was dedicated in his honor at Hillsboro's Central Park. My family and I attended, and we were moved to tears when Mayor Steve Callaway paid Alter tribute by saying:

> A bench is a rather common object, a relatively simple thing.
>
> Now, there are different types and styles of benches, but they have the same function. They serve the same purpose. They give respite. An opportunity to stop, rest,

observe. As you do, the most amazing thing happens. You watch, notice, and reflect.

And when there's somebody next to you, an even more amazing thing happens. You're at the same level. You're equals. You say hi, talk a bit, increase understanding, and maybe foster a relationship.

That's why a bench—this bench—in the heart of Orenco, is such an appropriate tribute to Alter Wiener.

Like a bench, Alter's book and his presentations gave us reasons to stop, pause, and reflect.

Like a bench, Alter brought us together to say hi, make us equals, increase understanding, and foster relationships.

I mentioned earlier that benches are common. That's the one significant difference, because Alter was anything but common. He was a once-in-a-lifetime person.

A month earlier, one of Alter's biggest dreams for me came true: I finally made it to the United States

Holocaust Memorial Museum. I had the great privilege of flying to Washington, DC, to give a speech and receive the Kay Family Award at the 2019 Anti-Defamation League's Concert Against Hate at the John F. Kennedy Center for the Performing Arts. Through the ADL, my family and I got a private tour of the museum. It was everything I hoped it would be, and I thought about Alter the entire time.

The museum in DC is far from the only place in the United States that memorializes those who suffered through or died in the Holocaust. Over thirty states in the United States have parks, memorials, and museums dedicated to these people, and in February 2020, I had the honor of visiting the Florida Holocaust Museum in St. Petersburg. The museum had invited me to be an honoree at their gala and speak on a panel about youth activism. Later that month, I attended BBYO's International Convention (BBYO is a Jewish teen movement with chapters around the world), and I shared my story with thousands of people so that they could learn how to create meaningful change in the world. Alter gave me that drive, and, in everything I do, I hope I can inspire it in others.

I miss Alter every single day. When I give a speech,

fundraise, attend a convention, walk into school, drink a smoothie, or work on this book, I feel his presence, and while it makes me sad for a few moments, I always end up smiling. Alter changed my perspective, my attitude, and my life in ways that will impact me forever. I will always be grateful for his friendship and example.

Alter's legacy lives on in my community and in his. After the bench ceremony, I worked to get the new library at Lakeridge Middle School named after him, and it's now called the Alter Wiener Memorial Library to recognize and honor the gift of education he gave to our school, community, and state.

You may not have an Alter in your life, but it doesn't matter. You have a voice. I'm a firm believer that each one of us is an activist in our own way. No matter who you are or where you come from, you can work to enact change and use your voice for good. Never let *anybody* limit you or tell you there's something you can't do. I believe passionately that no matter how young or old you are, you can be a difference maker. Never shy away from calling out injustices, educating, bringing people together, being a voice for unity, and making the impossible possible. Do everything that you can to make your vision for tomorrow a reality. There's really no better time to become a youth activist. Social media has given young people a platform that no other generation has had, and we have the power to use it for good.

My generation was born in the shadow of 9/11 and we have never lived without an American war. We have also never experienced a world without social media. We are more connected and aware of communities outside of our own than previous generations, so even though something bad might be happening "far, far away," we can't dismiss it so easily. Our elementary school, middle school, or high school years were shaped by lockdown drills, climate change, two United States–led wars in the Middle East, and a global pandemic. I wrote chapters of this book during the Oregon wildfires, when the smoke outside my house was so thick, I couldn't open the windows. I finished it while yet another wave of the Covid-19 pandemic raged around the world, the rate of hate crimes increased, and 2022 saw more school shootings than any other year (over three hundred!).

History is happening all around us. My generation

sees the world changing, and we wake up and want to act. I think the opportunities we've been afforded are so exciting, and I know Alter did, too. If there's anything I hope you get from this book, it's that you should never be afraid to stand up and fight against injustice, racism, antisemitism, and inequality—or fight *for* whatever it is you believe in. Your voice is strong, and it matters. Most of all, the world needs it. We can all be better, not bitter, no matter who we are or where we live.

Work hard. Always choose love over hate. Believe in the power your voice and actions have in making a difference. Stand up for what you believe in even if it feels like nobody is standing with you. Give people a reason to believe in the kindness and compassion of humanity.

Alter's stepmother said it best: Light a fire so that others can be warm, too.

AUTHOR'S NOTE

✦

THIS BOOK WOULDN'T EXIST IF ALTER'S HADN'T. Reading *From a Name to a Number* and then seeing him speak changed my life. I wish with all my heart that I could've written this story with Alter and not have to rely on my memory and his book to fill in some of the details from his life. I hope that reading this book will inspire you to read Alter's. And if you do, don't forget to leave a review. ☺

ACKNOWLEDGMENTS

✦

To my mom and dad, Carol and Ken Sarnowski. I would not be where I am today without you. Thank you for encouraging me to reach my dreams, allowing me to discover my interests and pursue my passions, putting up with my busy schedule without complaints, and chauffeuring me to my commitments before I had my license. I love you always.

To the most amazing teacher, mentor, and friend I will ever have, Alter Wiener. You changed my life. May your light and legacy live on forever. To Alter's family, thank you for sharing your father and grandfather with me and all who knew him.

To Ahboo (Aunt Sue), Grandma (Pat) Luft, and my

family from afar. Thank you for always believing in me and showing up for me. You've shown me what it means to lead with love, kindness, and compassion.

To my friends in Portland, Boston, and everywhere in between, you know who you are and you mean the world to me. Special shout-out to those who were by my side through it all: Amanda, Chanelle, Ethan, Flossie, Hannah, Jenna, Joey, Tina, and Ying. And to friends who became family: Ann, Tricia, the Bucks, the Spatzes, the Steinbergs, the Strealys, and the Thums.

To everyone who worked to make Senate Bill 664 a reality: Bob Barman, Senator Rob Wagner, Senator Janeen Sollman—thank you for listening to my voice. And to the incredible staff of the Oregon Jewish Museum and Center for Holocaust Education—Bob Horenstein, Eva and Les Aigner, Matthew Kahl, Rhonda Fink-Whitman, and Rob Hadley—and everyone else who helped the bill cross the finish line, this wouldn't have been possible without you.

To the teachers and mentors who sparked my intellectual curiosity and instilled within me an endless love of learning: Mrs. Mauritz, Mrs. Hutchison,

ACKNOWLEDGMENTS

———•———

Mr. McCarroll, Ms. Ryan, and Mr. Kelly. Thank you to the Lakeridge High School teachers and administration who cheered me on from home and understood my legislation-related absences.

To the literary dream team: my agent Peter Steinberg and staff, cowriter Sarah Durand, and everyone at Little, Brown Books for Young Readers. Thank you for all the long hours of editing, for the hundreds of phone calls and email exchanges, and for helping me share one of the most important aspects of my life with the world; you all are the best.

RESOURCES AND RECOMMENDED READING

◆

THERE ARE HUNDREDS—EVEN THOUSANDS—OF worthwhile programs and organizations and enriching books, movies, and websites about the Holocaust, genocides, and mass atrocities across the globe. Unfortunately, some of these books and movies are banned within schools, but the efforts of politicians and school boards can't stop their message from getting out. I couldn't possibly name all my favorites, but the ones I've learned the most from are listed here.

ORGANIZATIONS

The Student-Led Movement to End Mass Atrocities (STAND): This is a national youth-led organization that works to educate young people about mass atrocities and create a grassroots constituency focused on atrocity prevention. Since 2019, I have served on its Managing Committee. https://standnow.org.

USC Shoah Foundation: This organization, based at the University of Southern California (USC), has a mission to "develop empathy, understanding and respect through testimony," with programs, education, and an extensive visual history archive about the Holocaust. They hold conferences and events for teachers and students, have many amazing educational programs, and offer educators a way to bring survivor stories and testimony into their classrooms. In 2020, I was part of their William P. Lauder Junior Internship Program. https://sfi.usc.edu.

Echoes & Reflections: This terrific organization gives teachers the materials and tools to help students learn about the Holocaust. If you are a teacher and need lesson plans, ideas, or reading materials, they are there to help. https://echoesandreflections.org.

Facing History and Ourselves: With regional offices and global partners all over the world, this organization provides seminars, reading materials, and teaching tools for educators to learn and teach about everything from the Civil Rights Movement to genocides throughout history. https://www.facinghistory.org.

RESOURCES AND RECOMMENDED READING

———————•———————

PLACES TO VISIT

United States Holocaust Memorial Museum: I will always thank Alter for urging me to see this museum, and the Anti-Defamation League for providing me an opportunity to visit. If you're in our nation's capital, make time to go there. https://www.ushmm.org.

Auschwitz-Birkenau Memorial and Museum: More than 1.1 million people lost their lives within this camp's gates. While I haven't had a chance to visit, their website is full of resources including e-lessons, publications, library catalogs, and more. https://www.auschwitz.org/en.

Your local Holocaust/genocide/human rights museum: Dig a little deeper in your hometown, and you may find a museum dedicated to tolerance, fighting hate, and ending genocide. More are being built every year!

BOOKS

YOUNGER READERS

The Book Thief by Markus Zusak (Knopf Books for Young Readers, 2005).

The Boy in the Striped Pajamas by John Boyne (David Fickling Books, 2006).

The Boy on the Wooden Box by Leon Leyson (Atheneum Books for Young Readers, 2013).

RESOURCES AND RECOMMENDED READING

———•———

The Diary of a Young Girl by Anne Frank (Doubleday, 1952).

Gifts from the Enemy by Trudy Ludwig, illustrated by Craig Orback (White Cloud Press, 2014).

Maus I: A Survivor's Tale: My Father Bleeds History and *Maus II: A Survivor's Tale: And Here My Troubles Began* by Art Spiegelman (Pantheon, 1986, 1992).

Never Fall Down by Patricia McCormick (Balzer + Bray, 2012).

Number the Stars by Lois Lowry (Clarion Books, 1989).

Refugee by Alan Gratz (Scholastic, 2017).

White Bird: A Wonder Story (A Graphic Novel) by R. J. Palacio (Knopf Books for Young Readers, 2019).

OLDER READERS

94 Maidens by Rhonda Fink-Whitman (self-published, Dog Ear Publishing, 2012).

From a Name to a Number: A Holocaust Survivor's Autobiography by Alter Wiener (self-published, AuthorHouse, 2007).

An Indigenous Peoples' History of the United States by Roxanne Dunbar-Ortiz (Beacon Press, 2014).

Night by Elie Wiesel (Hill & Wang, 1960).

RESOURCES AND RECOMMENDED READING

———•———

Not on Our Watch: The Mission to End Genocide in Darfur and Beyond by Don Cheadle and John Prendergast (Hyperion, 2007).

Only Hope: A Survivor's Stories of the Holocaust by Felicia Bornstein Lubliner (Felabra Press, 2019).

Survival in Auschwitz (or *If This Is a Man*) by Primo Levi (The Orion Press, 1959).

CLAIRE SARNOWSKI spearheaded Senate Bill 664 (2019), which mandated Holocaust and genocide education in Oregon schools. She is a top fundraiser for the National MS Society and a national managing committee member for STAND: The Student-Led Movement to End Mass Atrocities. When she is not studying at Boston University, Claire resides in Lake Oswego, Oregon, with her parents. She invites you to follow her on Instagram @ClaireSarnowskiAuthor.

SARAH DURAND is a *New York Times* bestselling collaborator whose projects include *Renia's Diary: A Holocaust Journal* by the late Renia Spiegel and her surviving sister, Elizabeth Bellak; *Breakaway* by US women's soccer star Alex Morgan; and *My Shot* by WNBA All-Star Elena Delle Donne. Before she became a writer, Sarah was an editor for sixteen years. She lives in Brooklyn, New York, with her husband and two daughters. She invites you to visit her online at sarahdurandbooks.com.